The Guide To Becoming An Employee Benefits Know It All

By Denise Perkins, CEBS

Copyright

Preface

Not every job has an apprenticeship or other training program for entry-level professionals. And unless you are in a profession with a clearly defined skill set, learning how to do your job can be a loose process. Learning on the job, from colleagues, or your own mistakes is de facto corporate training at most organizations. Employee benefit professionals that want to perform at the highest level have to fill in the gaps of this relaxed training approach.

Becoming an *Employee Benefits Know It All* requires dedication to continuous learning. Learning new employee benefits concepts. Learning to communicate efficiently. Learning to use technology. Learning to problem solve in a world of grays. And learning to challenge the status quo...

This is *The Guide To Becoming An Employee Benefits Know It All*. It's chock full of advice, anecdotes, and resources to enhance the knowledge and credibility of new and developing benefit pros.

Table of Contents

INTRODUCTION..1

WELCOME TO THE WORLD OF EMPLOYEE BENEFITS.....................4

WHAT KIND OF EMPLOYEE BENEFIT PRO SHOULD YOU BE..................6

HOW TO LEARN ABOUT EMPLOYEE BENEFITS.............................9

READ, LISTEN, ASK QUESTIONS, TAKE A CLASS, REPEAT........................9

COMMUNICATION – SOME SKILLS MATTER MORE THAN OTHERS
....25

WRITTEN AND VERBAL COMMUNICATION SKILLS.....................................25

THINKING INSIDE THE TECHNOLOGY BOX...................................32

FIRST THINGS FIRST...33

WHAT TO DO WITH WHAT YOU KNOW.......................................41

DOCUMENTATION, CHECKLISTS, AND PROCEDURES – SAY WHAT!.....................41

INTERPERSONAL RELATIONSHIPS AT WORK – I LIKE AND
RESPECT YOU 46

THIRD-PARTY VENDORS AND SERVICE PROVIDERS –..............................47
WORKPLACE COLLEAGUES –..49

UPPING YOUR GAME AND ENHANCING YOUR CREDIBILITY.......55

YOU NEED TO KNOW SOMETHING ABOUT MEDICARE AND SOCIAL SECURITY
(SS)...56
YOU NEED TO KNOW HOW TO ASSIST ALL WORKERS...........................60
ANSWERING "HAVE YOU HEARD ABOUT" QUESTIONS.........................62
KEEP IT TO YOURSELF (KITY) 64

LEAVE MANAGEMENT – THE TOUGHEST EMPLOYEE BENEFITS
FUNCTION...67

TOP CHALLENGES OF LEAVE MANAGEMENT..68
CONQUERING LEAVE MANAGEMENT CHALLENGES..............................69

FINDING YOUR PLACE IN THE HR DEPARTMENT.......................72

IT'S TIME TO SHOW THEM WHAT YOU GOT..73

ONE STEP FORWARD, TWO STEPS BACK – FEELING
OVERWHELMED 75

I.   COPY, STUDY, IMPROVE 75
II.   ASK FOR HELP 78

THE STAGE IS YOURS BENEFIT PROS **80**

    HEALTH AND WELLNESS FAIRS 81
    NEW HIRE BENEFITS ORIENTATION 82
    ANNUAL BENEFITS OPEN ENROLLMENT 86

CLAIMS, CLAIMS, EVERYWHERE THERE'S CLAIMS… 89

    WHAT TO EXPECT FROM AN EMPLOYEE DISPUTING AN INSURANCE CLAIM 90
    GUIDELINES FOR ASSISTING AN EMPLOYEE WITH AN INSURANCE CLAIM
    DISPUTE 90
    LEARNING FROM EACH CLAIM DISPUTE INTERVENTION 91
    OTHER CLAIM DISPUTE CONSIDERATIONS 91
    WHEN TO BACK OUT OF A CLAIM DISPUTE 93

CONCLUSION **94**

RESOURCES **96**

EMPLOYEE BENEFITS SURVEYS...**97**

EMPLOYEE BENEFITS REFERENCES **99**

GOVERNMENT EMPLOYEE BENEFITS RESOURCES **102**

GOVERNMENT SURVEYS...**103**

EMPLOYEE BENEFITS PERIODICALS AND HEALTH CARE BOOKS
....**105**

EMPLOYEE BENEFITS ASSOCIATIONS.................................**107**

PROFESSIONAL CERTIFICATIONS AND DESIGNATIONS...............**109**

MORE EMPLOYEE BENEFITS RESOURCES **110**

Introduction

If you want a book that explains the difference between an HMO and PPO medical plan, this is not it. If you want to understand the Family and Medical Leave Act (FMLA), read the statutes. You can read thousands of resources that define employee benefit plans and laws. This Guide does not do any of that. However, if you want to know how to become a credible and respected employee benefit professional, this book is for you.

This Guide provides insights and tips on how to be an employee benefits pro instead of just acting like one. Yes. That's right. Many benefit pros fake their knowledge of employee benefits. They read scripts like actors. They get their scripts from various sources, including Supervisors, Colleagues, Brokers, Insurers, Third Party Vendors and Service Providers, Lawyers, and Accountants.

My opinion about fakers is not a criticism of benefit pros; it's an observation. And if you don't believe me, you can test my observation yourself. Here's how:

Ask a Benefits pro any employee benefits-related question. Allow them to answer and then ask—so what does that mean? If they struggle to provide an answer or repeat their initial response, their presentation is a script.

You may find my assessment of my fellow benefit pros unfair. What if their initial reply was "correct," and there was no other way to answer the question? My response to that type of thinking is welcome to the world of employee benefits, where there is always another way to answer a question. For one, not everyone has the exact comprehension and literacy level.

Many individuals struggle with health insurance literacy—this includes understanding what health insurance is and how to use it, as well as knowing basic health insurance terms like premium, deductible, and coinsurance. And according to a 2014 Kaiser Family Foundation survey, some groups have even lower levels of health insurance literacy, including young people, people with low levels of education, and the previously uninsured. Further, a 2011 Financial Literacy and Retirement Planning survey from the National Bureau of Economic Research shows that Americans may be even worse at understanding retirement plans and basic financial concepts than health insurance fundamentals. This survey found that young people, women, and minorities have the lowest financial literacy skills.

Second, clarifying your benefits messages requires fundamental knowledge and understanding of employee benefit plans and concepts. You can't fake this. Of course, some questions may require some reflection and research, but let me get back to you on that should not be your all-the-time response. But it will be if you are a faker.

A Benefits Know It All is familiar with the latest benefits surveys, trends, and case law and deeply understands insurance and other employee benefit plans. She does not have to get back to you. She can explore on the spot the difficulties her customers have with the information she presents. She can explain, not just recite.

It sounds harsh to call someone a professional faker. No one can know everything. You're right. But we can all know more, and being a Benefits Know It All is about continuous learning and improvement. The Japanese call it kaizen.

Nearly every Benefits Know It All starts their employee benefits career as a faker or script reader. I did. I had to because college did not prepare me to start administering benefit plans. And neither did my supervisors. My supervisors "trained" me on how to perform administrative tasks. They did not explain the "why" of the job and what it meant if I did not perform it well, and they never encouraged me to change or improve work processes.

And when it came to "learning" non-administrative tasks on the job, the training was even worse. Take, for example, the new hire employee benefits orientation. My training consisted of watching my supervisors (I had two in my first job in benefits) perform their version of an effective benefits orientation session. After a few dress rehearsals, it was my time to take the stage alone. I mimicked what I "learned" from my supervisors, stumbled when trying to answer questions, like what 401(k) means, and prayed no one would ask me any other questions I could not answer.

Oh, the humiliation! I knew I never wanted to feel that way again, not just for my pride but because I thought my customers deserved better than a script reader. So I got better at this employee benefits thing. Much better. But there's always room for improvement. Right?

You see, everyone needs health insurance and a retirement savings plan. Well, maybe the super-rich don't, but the rest of us do. Think of working in employee benefits as performing a public service. People need your help understanding some of the most complex issues they will ever have to confront. This Guide can help you meet their needs.

In this book, I'll focus on the many skills you need to learn and the resources you need to use to manage the employee benefits function of any organization. I'll also discuss many situations you will encounter and the skills and resources you need to address them all. And it's only fair that I share my experiences and failures as an employee benefits pro. I learned from them, and I'm betting you can too.

After reading this Guide you will learn...

• How to gain basic employee benefits knowledge
• Which skills every Benefits Know It All must master
• How to deal with challenging employee benefits issues and people
• How to obtain credibility and respect
• Why it is important to question the status quo

Welcome To The World Of Employee Benefits

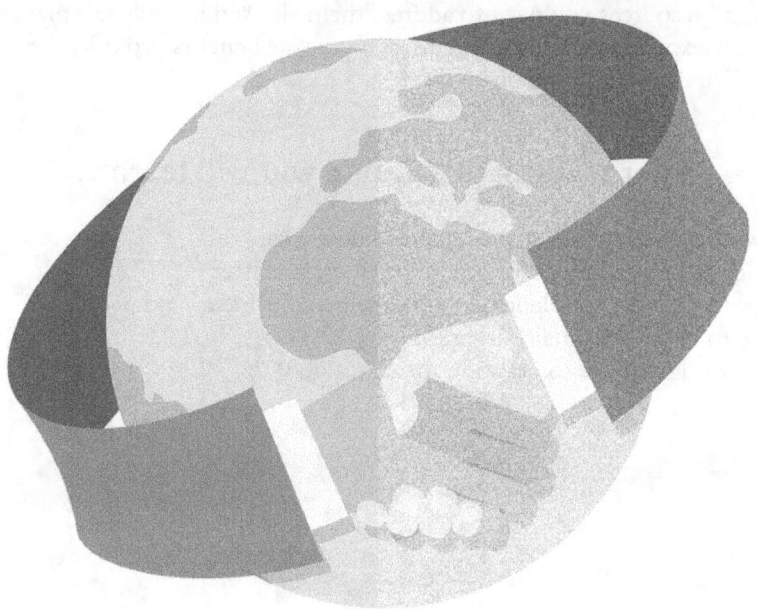

Let me tell you how I came to work in the employee benefits field, which I knew little about. Deciding on a career in human resources involved assessing the skills I thought I had, which ones I enjoyed employing, and how best to apply them.

It was the early 1990s, and I had a four-year degree in Business Management. Because my degree was general, I focused on the college courses I enjoyed the most and tried to find a job where I could use the knowledge and skills I learned. I liked learning computer applications like spreadsheets—an excellent skill for pension administration. I also enjoyed my introductory law class. Reading and commenting on case law was fun. I enjoyed many other courses, but my favorites were the computer, law, and public policy courses.

So with no real profession in mind but focused on skills I wanted to use, I searched job ads that required these skills. Eventually, a no-experience-required job as a Human Resources Assistant to the Pension and Compensation Manager and Benefits Manager came my way. Yep, I had two direct supervisors for my first professional job. At first, I struggled with the arrangement because of their different work styles—one obsessed with detail and the other not at all focused on the details. Still, I felt and still feel fortunate to have had the opportunity to learn all areas of the employee benefits function so early in my career.

My detail-oriented supervisor taught me the importance of being precise and thorough when performing tasks. I also learned that learning the benefits craft doesn't just take place at work. He taught me that reading financial news helped in understanding and managing pension plans. And due to his obsession with creating formulas in Microsoft Excel, I learned that using Excel was required. In sum, the man taught me how to learn on and off the job.

My not-so-detail-oriented supervisor taught me a few things, also. She taught me that a friendly and caring personality is as important as technical knowledge. However, on occasion, I found her work style frustrating. She was often unorganized and, at times, distracted by other commitments.

She would assign me a task, leave out essential information, or never follow up when she received additional information. I recall preparing premium statements (insurance bills) and her always "forgetting" to tell me if a retiree passed away and required removal from the Plan and account. I would have to make an amended statement, and, of course, the Finance folks cutting the check (this was the age of checks and not wire transfers) assumed it was my mistake. Not good for my credibility.

Still, she had some positive qualities that my detail-oriented manager did not have and that I admired. She was easygoing, kind, and relaxed with workers at all levels of the organization. She treated everyone respectfully and welcomed them to her office for a visit. She could sit and focus on who was in front of her. When they left her office, she was hard-pressed to recall all the details of the encounter.

Bottom line. I adapted to my supervisors' work styles and decided which characteristics I wanted to adopt and which I did not. It was an excellent and, again, fortunate introduction to the world of employee benefits. However, I had much more to learn before putting down the script. First, I had to develop a rock-solid understanding of benefits laws and employee benefits, including medical, dental, vision, life, and disability insurance, as well as retirement savings plans and tax issues. Second, I had to evaluate and improve my communication skills—verbal and written. Third, I had to use my growing knowledge to improve work processes and increase my value to the benefits function. Fourth, I had to bring it all together and stop thinking about employee benefits administration as performing disjointed tasks.

What Kind Of Employee Benefit Pro Should You Be

Benefit Generalist or Specialist?

My introduction to employee benefits was near perfect. I had the privilege of participating in every benefits function. Retirement, performance management, compensation, leave management, health, life, disability, dental, vision, retiree health. Oh, I also helped with recruiting—writing ads, coordinating and participating in interviews, and checking references. And I worked for nonprofit, private, public, and union-based companies—the best of all worlds.

This broad introduction to the world of employee benefits administration allowed me to zero in on the functions I enjoyed performing and the ones I did not. And although I continued to do it all, there were some functions I devoted more time and effort to learning. But not everyone will have my introduction to benefits. Sometimes a route is chosen for you based on the employer's needs.

Some employee benefits jobs only allow you to work with health and welfare plans; some compensation programs or retirement plans only. Trying to learn other functions outside your job description may be difficult for several reasons.

• You may have coworkers that are afraid of others learning how to perform their job
• You may have a supervisor or manager that prefers a strict division of duties
• You may work for a company that does not have a comprehensive benefits program

It's up to you to decide whether to be a benefits generalist or specialist. Just know that you may have to convince others to let you in on assignments outside your regular job duties. And you may have to engage in some job-hopping to do what you want. There are advantages and disadvantages to either approach. However, being a benefits generalist does not mean you only know a little bit about everything—you can learn a lot about everything benefits-related. And the reverse is also true. Being a benefits specialist does not mean you only know how to do one thing. It is up to you how much you learn and how you put that knowledge to work.

"At least we are consistently inconsistent."

Issue-Focused or Individual-Focused Benefit Pros?

Believe it or not, there are benefit pros that dislike interacting with employees. They cringe whenever the phone rings or someone knocks on their office door. It's not that they don't want to help workers with their employee benefits questions; they just don't want to do it so intimately. They are the Issue-focused Benefit Pros.

Then there are the benefit pros that can't get enough one-on-one employee interaction. They spend hours each day talking to employees about benefits and non-benefits issues. They pride themselves on knowing the most intimate details about employees. Call them the Individual-focused Benefit Pros.

Neither pro is better than the other. The way most pros approach the job has more to do with work style and personality than any other factor. Just know that your work style may impact how you are treated in- and outside of the department. Some people will appreciate your style, and others will not. It is up to you to adapt your style or move on to a workplace that suits your style better.

Status Quo or Revolutionary Benefit Pros?

Most benefit pros are in the status quo camp. They don't question the way things are done. Accepting things as they are and not making waves is easier than challenging norms. They think that treating everyone the same is fair. They believe there is only one way to do something—the job is black or white. They risk being consistently wrong about things they are 100% sure are correct.

Revolutionary benefit pros know that they work in a world of grays. Treating everyone the same is easy and forces you to say "no" when you should be looking for a way to say "yes." They don't believe in; that's the way we've always done it, so that's the way [it] should be done now. They question the status quo and look for ways to enhance their profession.

Revolutionary benefit pros also make their opinions about workplace benefits known outside the organization. They write articles, create blogs, and join organizations that promote their profession and question its purpose.

How To Learn About Employee Benefits

High schools seldom teach students basic life skills such as financial literacy and risk management. Parents also neglect to pass on what they know about finance and insurance to their children. And university HR degree programs seldom include separate insurance or benefits management classes. No wonder most young workers, including those entering the employee benefits profession, struggle to understand health insurance.

When I started working in employee benefits, it was no different for me—I had a general idea of what insurance was, but that was it. So I had to read, listen, ask lots of questions, and take a few classes.

Read, Listen, Ask Questions, Take A Class, Repeat

Read

One of my favorite quotes about reading comes from American writer Tomie dePaola, who said, "Reading is important, because if you can read, you can learn anything about everything and everything about anything."

Reading and understanding what you read is the most important skill of any Benefits Know It All. So if reading is not your thing or you vowed never to read anything heavy again after graduating from college, don't choose the employee benefits profession as a career. You won't enjoy it.

What To Read. Deciding what to read in your quest to learn more about employee benefits takes thought and planning. When I started in the field, access to reliable benefit plan information mainly came in the form of summaries of case law, a few chapters in business textbooks, handouts at seminars, and insurance certification courses. In sum, benefits information was sparse, and you read whatever was available. Only schools and large workplaces had Internet access. Home-based Internet access was rare in the early 1990s.

Today that is no longer the case. In fact, there is too much information about health insurance, employee benefits administration, tax-favored benefits, and retirement savings plans on the Internet. Every stakeholder in the game has a website or blog filled to the brim with employee benefits information, including insurance companies, law firms, human resource management and employee benefits groups and associations, brokers and advisers, and freelance writers. Even the mainstream media consistently writes about workplace benefits like health insurance and retirement plans.

The challenge for new and seasoned employee benefit professionals is to sort through the avalanche of benefits information because not all of it is good or accurate. And the best way to read just the good stuff is to use only reputable sources. What is a reputable source?

A reputable source:

• Has educational expertise in the subject matter
• Focuses on facts supported by evidence
• Cites other reputable sources such as academic research and surveys
• Is known as a reputable source

For example, Forbes Magazine is a reputable source for financial and retirement-related articles; Forbes.com is not. Forbes Magazine articles are written by hired or contracted subject matter experts and are reviewed and edited by others. Unedited Forbes.com articles can come from anyone.

However, that does not mean you shouldn't read a retirement plan article posted on Forbes.com. If the headline grabs you, read it. It's okay to read a non-expert's opinion of the latest retirement plan regulation; just give it the appropriate weight.

Reputable Online Employee Benefits Publications

The great thing about the below list of benefits resources is that most have robust websites, produce a daily or weekly e-newsletter you can subscribe to, or a blog you can follow. Check them all out and add your own. But remember, every resource you use has an agenda. There's nothing wrong with having an agenda; however, you must understand the intent of the publications you read. Understanding intent allows you to build a database of resources that cover many different perspectives. For example:

A publication may have a conservative or progressive point of view about legislative changes such as health care reform or,

A publication may have a financial interest in promoting a concept or product (for example, a trade publication may not favor government regulation that could jeopardize its members' profits)

Government Resources

• Code of Federal Regulations (CFR - ecfr.gov)
• Department of Labor (dol.gov)
• ELAWS Health Benefits Advisor
• Employee Benefits Security Administration (EBSA)
• Healthcare.gov
• Internal Revenue Code (irs.gov)
• Medicare (Medicare.gov)
• Office of Personnel Management (OPM)
• Social Security Administration (SSA.gov)

Health & Welfare Plan Resources

• BenefitsLink - Health & Welfare Plans Newsletter

- BenefitsPro
- Employee Benefits News
- Federal Employees Health Benefits Program
- FierceHealthFinance

Retirement Savings Plans Resources

- 401khelpcenter
- BenefitsLink - Retirement Plans Newsletter
- BrightScope
- FeeX
- Freeerisa.benefitspro
- Jemstep
- Motley Fool
- Pensions & Investments

Other Benefit plan Resources

- American Association of Retired Persons (AARP)
- Bloomberg BNA (Bureau of National Affairs-HR)
- Cypen & Cypen Newsletter (public sector benefits)
- eHealthInsurance
- Employee Benefits Research Institute (EBRI)
- Healthcare Bluebook
- International Foundation of Employee Benefit Plans (IFEBP)
- Kaiser Family Foundation
- Law Firm Benefits Blogs –websites of law firms that have an ERISA practice group
- PlanSponsor
- SavingForCollege (529 Plans)
- Society for Human Resource Management (SHRM)
- SCOTUSBlog (Supreme Court of the United States)

Benefit Plan Documents

Setting up employee benefit plans requires the production of a lot of plan materials. Once these plans go live, employers must create, distribute and maintain multiple plan documents. Insurance companies and third-party vendors, and service providers work with employers to develop these documents. Employees receive some of these documents automatically and some upon request.

These documents are important from both a legal and employee education perspective. Employers are required by law to have an SPD and Plan Document for each Plan. Employers must administer their plans in accordance with the terms and conditions outlined in the Plan Document. The integrity of these documents is the top priority of every employee benefits department. NOT!

Non-existent, outdated, or ignored is a good way to describe the state of the benefit plan documents in many organizations. It is the dirty little secret of the employee benefits profession. Below are some of the reasons why.

Why Are Benefit Plan Documents Neglected or Ignored

• Some organizations do not have professional benefits staff and do not know what is required

• Some organizations do have professional benefits staff and do not know what is required

• Some organizations believe that the documents they receive from the insurer or third-party administrator are the only ones they need and that they are complete and accurate

• Some employee benefits department heads believe in a once-and-done approach to plan documentation, never bothering to update outdated information, or they forget to update plan changes and amendments

• Some employee benefits department heads believe that there is little risk of noncompliance

• Some senior managers do not want to pay for the necessary legal services to draft or review plan documents such as the SPD and Plan Document

• Benefits department heads and the people they report to want the flexibility and discretion to administer the plans as they see fit. And plan documents can get in the way of that

Types of Employee Benefit Plan Documents

• Summary Annual Report (SAR)

• Summary of Benefits and Coverage (SBC) – usually a two- to four-page summary of basic plan features and costs

• Certificate of Coverage (COC) – detailed description of the Plan's benefits; usually provided by the insurer

• Summary Plan Description (SPD) – usually includes the COC plus the required ERISA language and special notices such as HIPAA Privacy Notice, Medicare Part D Notice of Creditable Coverage, Medicaid and CHIP, Newborn and Mother's Protection Act, Special Enrollment Rights, Women's Health Cancer Rights Act. It is basically a summary of the plan document meant for employee consumption

• Plan Document – technical Document of little use to employees. Its purpose is to serve as a guide to the plan administrator (employer) in how to carry out the provisions of the Plan

Other benefit plan-related documents you need to know include:

• Insurance Contract or Agreement
• Corporate Resolution
• Explanation of Benefits (EOB) Statement
• Medical Child Support Order (MCSO)
• Qualified Domestic Relations Order (QDRO)
• Consolidate Omnibus Budget Reconciliation Act (COBRA) notices

Obtaining and Maintaining Plan Documents

• Make a list of all of your employee benefit plans in Excel

• Inventory the plan documents you have for all of these plans (at a minimum, make sure you have a Summary Plan Description (SPD) for each health and welfare plan and retirement plan)

• Review plan documents for completeness and accuracy. Are all the required legal notices and other language included in the Document? You can obtain model notices from the Dept. of Labor (DOL) website or purchase one from a private publisher like Thompson Media Group. You can also go online and view other employers' SPDs. Many employers post their SPDs online for easy access by their employees, but these documents are often accessible to anyone

• Make sure you have a signed contract or agreement for each benefit plan and third-party contract. If you do not have one, email your insurance rep. or TPA to request a signed copy. Someone signed one at some time, and you can be certain that the insurer and TPA kept their signed copies

• Make sure you have a signed company resolution establishing each Plan. The Finance Department may maintain these resolutions, so start there first. If no one at the company has one, draft one and get it signed. You can find sample resolutions online (e.g., Corporate Resolution: Establishment of 401(k) Plan… toolbox.bpas.com/images/uploads/SampleBoardResolution.doc)

• Update each Plan Document to reflect real-world plan administration

• Make sure you have at least a digital copy of each plan document

• Hire an attorney to review your Plan Documents and SPDs or create a "wrap" document

• Review your benefit plan documents at the start of each fiscal or calendar year and make any needed updates

If you need help finding plan documents in-house:

1. Contact each insurer and plan service provider to have the latest version sent to you.
2. In fact, call them all anyway to make sure you have the latest versions on file.
3. Get a digital copy.
4. Get copies of benefit plan-related documents like EOBs, MCSOs, QDROs, etc.
5. Ask the insurer to walk you through an EOB, or ask the firm's benefits counsel to explain QDROs and MCSOs.
6. Write explanatory notes on the form.

Now, read this documentation. Read it all. Print it. Place it in a binder for future reference. It will serve as the backup to the digital versions you have in PDF format.

Benefits Regulations and Laws

There is no substitute for reading federal and state laws that regulate employee benefit plans. You should bookmark the websites of the Department of Labor (DOL), Employee Benefits Security Administration (EBSA), Equal Employment Opportunity Commission (EEOC), Health and Human Services (HHS), and Internal Revenue Service (IRS).

"We have all kinds of Regulatory Guidelines floating around."

You can also bookmark specific pages of benefits laws and regulations like the Family and Medical Leave Act (FMLA). Also, don't forget state benefits laws like unemployment compensation, workers' compensation, states COBRA, and employee and family leave laws. Every state has a website that includes the full text of the statutes, frequently asked questions (FAQs), and contact information.

Federal Employee Benefits Laws:

• ADA – Americans With Disabilities Act

- ADEA – Age Discrimination in Employment Act
- COBRA – Consolidated Omnibus Budget Reconciliation Act
- ERISA – Employee Retirement Income Security Act
- FMLA – Family and Medical Leave Act
- GINA – Genetic Information Nondiscrimination Act
- HIPAA – Health Insurance Portability and Accountability Act
- MHPA – Mental Health Parity Act
- MHPAEA – Mental Health Parity and Addiction Equity Act
- NMHPA – Newborns' and Mothers' Health Protection Act
- PPACA (aka ACA and Obamacare) – Patient Protection And Affordable Care Act
- WHCRA – Women's Health And Cancer Rights Act

What Else Should You Read?

If you decide to take an employee benefits course or attend a seminar, you should of course read all assigned readings and handouts. However, you should never try to get all your employee benefits knowledge from courses, certifications, and seminars. Also, consider the reputation of these resources as you would any other resource.

Three more things about reading...

1) ***Read*** about health insurance and retirement planning around the world. There are similarities and differences in how countries provide health care and retirement resources. Learn how foreign health benefits programs differ from U.S. programs. Understanding how other countries administer health insurance plans can also provide ideas for improving your work processes. And who knows, you may someday work in a foreign employee benefits office, and you'll already have a basic understanding of their health care and retirement systems.

2) ***Read*** about subjects with a close or tangential relationship to the employee benefits function. For example:

- financial and investment news including tracking the markets
- medical and pharmaceutical research
- health care and retirement plan services technology and innovation
- general business news (mergers, acquisitions, layoffs, product announcements, disaster response, etc.)

Google Alerts

It's a great idea to track benefits topics on social media and set up Google Alerts for employee benefits-related subjects such as health, dental, and vision insurance, health insurance and retirement plan surveys, employee benefits surveys, life insurance, flexible spending accounts, health savings accounts, retirement plans, 401(k) plans, retirement plan surveys, Obamacare, health care reform, wellness programs and more. These Google Alerts can direct you to other published resources.

RSS Feeds

Want to read the latest articles and blog posts on a specific employee benefits topic? Sign up for the RSS Feed of a reputable online source. For example, to keep track of the latest health care reform news, I subscribe to the Kaiser Health News (KHN) health care reform RSS feed (http://feeds.kaiserhealthnews.org/topics/healthreform). There are several other employee benefits-related feeds you can set up with KHN and other sources.

Note: Not everyone is into RSS Feed technology, so who knows how long it will survive? But it can be an excellent resource for curating a lot of information with little effort.

3) *Read* about local, national, and world events. You can learn so many things from general news from all over the world related to your job as a benefits professional. For example, employees may have safety concerns about workers traveling to places experiencing a health scare. Remember the Ebola crisis of 2014? I can't help but wonder if the medical personnel at Texas Health Presbyterian Hospital that first treated Eric Duncan knew about the Ebola outbreak raging in Africa. Duncan allegedly told them that he had recently traveled from Liberia; if true, why didn't they at least consider that he had an Ebola infection, an international crisis at the time? Were they unaware of the Ebola breakout? Did HR not provide the appropriate communication and training?

If you don't get it by now, let me be more precise: **you can't be a** *Benefits Know It All* **without reading. A lot.**

TIP: When starting out in the employee benefits profession, read summaries of benefits laws. These summaries can come from the federal departments responsible for enforcing the laws and regulations or reputable law firms specializing in employee benefits. Wait to tackle reading the text of the entire regulation.

Listen

Everyone knows that listening skills help you learn and grow. We can all be better listeners; it's just so hard. Listening is more challenging when you don't understand the subject.

Reality Check: As an employee benefit professional, new or seasoned, you will participate in discussions that are, at first, over your head.

Employee benefits administration is broad and complex. Some benefit plans are easier to understand than others for certain people. Retirement plans may be your thing or plan communication; meanwhile, you struggle to understand the different types of life insurance plans. So, you may decide to tune out on any discussions involving things you find complex or boring, but that would be a mistake for any employee benefit professional.

As you start out in the benefits field, most meetings you attend will include new subject matter. You will feel intimidated and think you can't learn this stuff. You can. But first, you have to listen to what others say about employee benefits. Eventually, your knowledge of benefits will increase. That's if you learn to listen with the goal of understanding what you hear and; seek out opportunities to listen to knowledgeable people in the field.

<u>Who To Listen To</u>: The employee benefits administration function is unique in that benefit professionals, even entry-level ones, communicate regularly with many professionals in and outside the workplace. You will meet and speak regularly with the following:

• Insurance company representatives for every benefit plan
• Brokers
• Third-party administrators
• Service providers
• Record keepers
• Attorneys
• Financial advisers (investment, accounting, actuarial)

Some of these titles are used interchangeably but the point is that benefit pros have a lot of potential teachers. When you first start out in the field, just listening in on conversations among these people can provide a wealth of knowledge.

TIP: Even if you think you have good listening skills, you should look for ways to improve them. Consider taking a course, attending a seminar, or purchasing a listening skills app (for example, Elevate) to develop and practice listening skills.

Ask Questions

As an employee benefit professional, you will have many opportunities to exercise your voice.

• You will answer lots of questions
• You will present information at meetings
• You will talk to vendors and service providers over the phone and in person
• You will discuss strategy with supervisors and peers

But one of the most important things benefit pros can and should do with their voice is to ask questions. A mistake many benefit professionals make is to make assumptions because they want to avoid asking questions. Some people feel that asking questions makes you look less knowledgeable—too bad they don't understand that looking less knowledgeable is better than being less knowledgeable.

Asking questions is how you learn and keep learning. Here are two instances where asking questions is imperative:

1) When you don't know or fully understand a topic
2) When you need more details to better understand a topic

Wouldn't you rather be known as the benefits pro who asked "too many" questions than the benefits pro that consistently provided incomplete or wrong answers because you didn't ask enough questions? However, it is important to balance asking too few questions with asking too many. Another important thing to remember when asking questions is to be neutral in your question asking—meaning don't be emotional, judgmental, or accusatory. Respect people's time and privacy, and acknowledge that not everyone communicates well. You're not engaging in combat; you're trying to learn by asking a few questions.

TIP: Sometimes, it is easier and more comfortable to make assumptions rather than ask questions. It's not. Correcting mistakes is a lot more challenging than asking questions.

- Never act on limited information
- Never make assumptions
- Never refuse to ask follow-up questions
- Never ask more than you need to understand and act on an issue

Take A Class

I know when you graduated from college, you promised yourself that you would never, ever take another academic course. Well, that's up to you, but if you want to become a Benefits Know It All, taking a few insurance courses could help.

You can get several certifications that will improve your finance, risk, and insurance knowledge—the heart of employee benefits administration. Here are a few to consider that you can do self-study or classroom style:

- AGI – Associate in General Insurance – (3 courses)
- ARM – Associate in Risk Management – (3 courses)
- CEBS – Certified Employee Benefits Specialist (8 courses)
- CMS – Compensation Management Specialist (3 CEBS courses)
- GBA – Group Benefits Associate (3 CEBS courses)
- RPA – Retirement Plans Associate (3 CEBS courses)
- SHRM-CP – Society for Human Resource Management Certified Professional
- SHRM-SCP – Society for Human Resource Management Senior Certified Professional

However, keep in mind that not all benefits certifications are created equal. There are certification courses for beginners and seasoned professionals. For example, The Institutes® three (3)-course insurance and risk management Associate programs include courses any benefits newbie can handle. They are an excellent place to start if you have no insurance or risk management knowledge. On the other end of the course, difficulty spectrum are the CEBS and CEBS-related certifications, with the SHRM courses somewhere in the middle.

Even if you think you are a good student, pursuing the SHRM and CEBS certifications with less than two to three years of working with employee benefits is probably not the best use of your time and effort. You may pass the exams, but how much of what you "learn" will you understand or retain? It always amazes and disappoints me when I see help-wanted ads for entry- and other lower-level benefits professional jobs requiring a SHRM or CEBS certification. Seasoned insurance brokers, health insurance and financial managers, and executives struggle to complete the CEBS courses and pass eight (8) exams to receive the designation. Many of them fail to attain it.

Confession: My detailed-oriented supervisor from my first job was a Pension and Compensation Manager. He enrolled in the CEBS certification program before hiring me. He had years of experience in retirement and compensation management; which is about sixty percent of the CEBS coursework. However, health insurance was not his area of expertise. He often spoke about the coursework's difficulty—even the retirement and compensation-related stuff. Still, he thought it a good idea to require the other Benefits Administrator and me to start taking CEBS courses.

So, long story short, we confronted him halfway through our first CEBS course with an, "Are you serious?" He relented, and about ten years later I got my CEBS certification on my own. I learned a lot from that guy, but he was crazy to think that a person with no employee benefits knowledge or experience could or should take high-level CEBS courses.

Seminars, Maybe?

Okay, so you're not interested in taking even the three courses and exams by The Institutes®. You want something that takes less time and effort, and maybe, you'll do some coursework later. You might think you can learn all you need about employee benefits by attending a few related seminars and reading a few benefits publications. I hear you. I disagree, but I do hear you.

I am not a big fan of seminars. That's heretical for modern human resource professionals. The human resource profession loves seminars, and that includes the benefits function.

More on seminars...

Throughout my career in employee benefits, I mainly attended seminars because I was instructed to, not by choice. I realized early in my career that I did not learn much from attending seminars. They were a way for me to get a free lunch, eat cookies, and drink water all day. I like cookies and water. I also enjoyed the interaction with other professionals.

And, yes, I did learn something by attending seminars. Seminars provide good information about the latest benefits-related case law and what new laws and regulations are on the horizon. But a seminar on organizing my employee benefits files—interesting ideas that I'm never going to implement.

In a nutshell, the problem with seminars is that they are more entertaining than educational. **Case in point**:

My detailed-oriented supervisor from my first employee benefits job took the entire human resource department to a seminar on kaizen. Kaizen, or the study of continuous improvement, was the latest business management fad receiving attention in business research publications like the Harvard Business Review (HBR). The seminar was in my hometown of Philadelphia so I was already in a good mood when we met at the site of the seminar.

As each seminar attendee entered the room, the presenter introduced himself and asked our names. You know what's coming next because this probably happened to you too! Well, for those of you who don't know what I'm about to say, here goes:

Once everyone was seated at the seminar, the presenter went around the room and said hello to everyone by name. There were over 30 people in attendance. It was amazing, and we all squealed with glee. He then told us how he could remember all of our names—he repeated them two to three times when he introduced himself and noticed one unique item we were wearing.

So what do you think I learned at the seminar? How to introduce kaizen into my work and professional life or remember a person's name? The latter but learning to remember someone's name is a great and important skill, so this was a seminar I enjoyed.

For the record, I'm not against learning about employee benefits by attending seminars. I have learned a thing or two at seminars. And I've met some great presenters and other pros at these events. But for the most part, I think seminars focus too much on entertaining the crowd and not enough on learning.

TIP: Taking general insurance courses at the start of your employee benefits career is worth the time and effort. Is it fun to attend school while working full-time? No. However, you can take online and self-study courses at your own pace. Also, wait until you have several years of experience before attempting higher-level certifications. You can also attend seminars to stay on top of the latest employee benefits trends and case law.

Communication – Some Skills Matter More Than Others

Reading may be the essential first step in your journey to becoming a top employee benefits pro. Still, your writing and verbal communication and technology skills will validate your status.

Written and Verbal Communication Skills

Nearly every job ad includes a "must have excellent communication skills" requirement. Sometimes the wording is more specific, such as, "must have excellent *written and verbal* communication skills." Regardless of the language, all applicants claim to meet this qualification. However, the ability to speak or write a sentence does not make you an excellent communicator. Besides, you don't get to say you are an excellent communicator; other people do. And not everyone will evaluate your communication skills the same.

Some people rate an excellent communicator as someone that eliminates all the "ums," "uhs," and "likes" from their speech. Others praise communicators that write descriptively and have an extensive vocabulary. Such commendations usually point to the communication style, not the communication itself. Be wary of praise that focuses on your communication style only. Besides, some scientists think that "ums" and "uhs" are natural part of speech that does not detract from the message but help listeners focus more on what you say. We're not a robot.

It's not that communication style is not important. It is. Well-written or well-spoken communication elevates the message by making it more straightforward. However, at the heart of good communication skills is the ability to explain an issue in a way others can understand. **Excellent and effective communication skills result from the clarity of thought, ability to explain, AND a polished communication style**. Attaining excellent and effective communication skills requires continuous practice and evaluation. As an employee benefit professional, you will have many opportunities to rehearse.

Write This Way...

Human Resource departments tend to have designated writers for all department communication. Often the designees are the heads of the different HR functions. Sometimes non-managers provide first drafts of specific communication, and managers edit the drafts. The editing may stop there or get bumped up to the head of HR for final approval. This process assumes that writing skills improve as pay and job titles go up. They don't.

Writing skills get better through practice. Also, writing often is not the same as practicing your writing skills.

Here are some basic ways to improve your writing skills:

• Read and do the exercises in the Princeton Review's Grammar Smart, Word Smart and Write Smart books (you may remember these books from high school English class. They are updated periodically and can serve as an excellent refresher for business writing)

• Use a thesaurus (So important!)

• Read materials written by great writers (my favorite author is David McCullough; my favorite daily read is Vox.com)

• Use online resources for free writing tips from famous authors and other writers. Also, check out writing blogs and websites (that's blogs about writing)

• Write short sentences using words with few syllables

• Do not use jargon, instead define what you mean and give an example (Instead of just using the words deductible and coinsurance, provide an example of what these terms mean in the real world. Break your example down into short sentences or use a chart)

• Communicate at the average person's reading and grade level. (The literature on literacy is all over the place, but some research claims that the average person reads at a 7th-grade reading level. Considering that the adult illiteracy rate in the U.S. is in the double digits, that's a fair guestimate.) Use a tool like Microsoft Word Flesch-Kincaid Grade Level and Reading Ease—open a Word document and go to Tools/Spelling and Grammar/Options/Show Readability Statistics

• Focus on one or two topics at a time

• Edit and Rearrange

• Read and Write every day

Confession: It took me years to figure out that I was not a good writer. In my defense, everyone told me I was. The "very well-written" comments were at the top of my research papers and reports, and the "this is really good" comments from colleagues and supervisors. And other people wanted me to edit their writing. So, yeah, I thought I was a good writer. I wasn't. I'm still working on it.

I know, too much detail. Confess already.

One year I sent out a detailed open enrollment announcement explicitly letting people know what they had to do to continue participating in our company's cafeteria plan. They save money when participating in the plan; they don't if they don't. Over 40% of workers did not reenroll in the plan and had less money in their paychecks because of it. Of course, they blamed me.

They were angry. I was angry. I told them exactly what they needed to do to continue receiving the savings and they didn't do it, and they blamed me. It took me years to accept some responsibility for what happened. I shared the blame because I assumed everyone would read the announcement AND understand it as I intended.

After that, I always had someone unfamiliar with benefit plans read my work. I shortened the length of every announcement and used more bulleted lists. I realized that I was only a good writer if people understood my writing.

TIP: As an employee benefits professional, you will write lots of emails, letters, and summaries. At a minimum, your writing cannot include spelling, grammar, or punctuation errors. At its most effective, your writing will be brief and precise. Do not assume that because you find employee benefits interesting and easy to understand that anyone else will. They won't.

Talk This Way...

You may be surprised to learn that most human resource departments view the benefits function as a back-office operation. Yeah, many HR department heads prefer we pop up once yearly during open enrollment. They don't think we have the same interpersonal skills as HR generalists and recruiters. Meanwhile, employees seek us out for assistance more often than any other HR professional.

Despite the benefits function's ranking within the HR department, benefit pros often speak with employees at all levels of the organization and their family members. And let's not forget all of the external third-party vendors and service providers (insurers, brokers, administrators, lawyers, etc.) you will interact with regularly via email and phone. These relationships will help you sharpen your verbal communication skills.

That Style Thing Again...

Speaking may be easier than writing for most of us, but effective verbal communication skills are about more than just talking. Effective verbal communication is a skill that requires learning and practice. It requires the

ability to convey information clearly and concisely, to listen, as well as quick thinking, and thoughtful responses. It's like searching through a database, retrieving only the relevant information, and relaying it, but not in a robotic way.

Many people associate excellent verbal communication skills with style.

• Do they speak with confidence and authority?
• Do they have an extensive vocabulary?
• Do they speak without stammering?
• Do they speak with a smile in their voice?

As with writing, your verbal communication style can make your words easier to understand. It's difficult to understand someone who stammers, no matter how knowledgeable they are. The reverse is also true (a personable presenter who does not have command of the subject matter). Again, effective verbal communication combines both style and the ability to explain clearly and in a few words.

Here are some basic ways to improve your verbal communication skills:

• Breathe
• Smile – in person and on the phone
• Have a solid understanding of the subject matter
• Focus (show some interest and energy)
• Pace yourself
• Write a script or outline and read through it a few times
• Use humor (lighten up; don't be so serious)
• Stay on point and be concise and clear
• Listen
• Anticipate questions and prepare a response
• Practice
• Focus on those style things – limit the "ums" and such, no monotone or slurring speech, no crossing the arms and rolling the eyes… It's quite natural to add fillers—like, um, and uh to your speech, and speaking should be natural. Some recent research even suggests that saying "um" helps cue an audience for what's coming next, which makes them more likely to listen with care

That is quite the list, so concentrate on a few things at a time. Trust me; you will have many opportunities to practice your verbal communication skills. For me, the most important verbal skills to remember are to breathe, smile, listen, and maintain focus. Knowing the subject matter well helps me work on the other things I could do better.

Confession: I have more work-related verbal communication fails than I care to remember. It can happen when relaying complex employee benefits information. We benefit pros get so caught up in the jargon and in trying to relay so much information, that we forget or change the objective of the communication. Here's just one of many examples of when my verbal communication skills failed badly [Another open enrollment blunder]:

At an annual open enrollment meeting I told employees and their spouses that their health insurance premiums were increasing **(but not as much as they would if we did not change insurance carriers)**. To my surprise, nearly everyone present interpreted my statement to mean that their premiums were not rising. To this day, I do not understand exactly how they interpreted my explanation to mean the opposite of what I said. Still, in all future enrollment meetings, I told attendees that their insurance premiums were increasing by 3%.

What did I do wrong in the first meeting? My statement was too long, which made it unclear. But I so wanted everyone to know how much money I saved them! Or maybe I should have added the word "by," as in *"but not by as much...."*

TIP: It's not about you... When you find yourself discussing the same subjects repeatedly, it is easy to think you're an expert--that you know your stuff. You're a smooth operator (true story: I once heard the head of HR refer to himself this way). But thinking about the recipient is the best way to improve your verbal communication skills. Keep the focus on them. You have more work to do if they don't understand your explanation. Keep practicing.

Thinking Inside The Technology Box

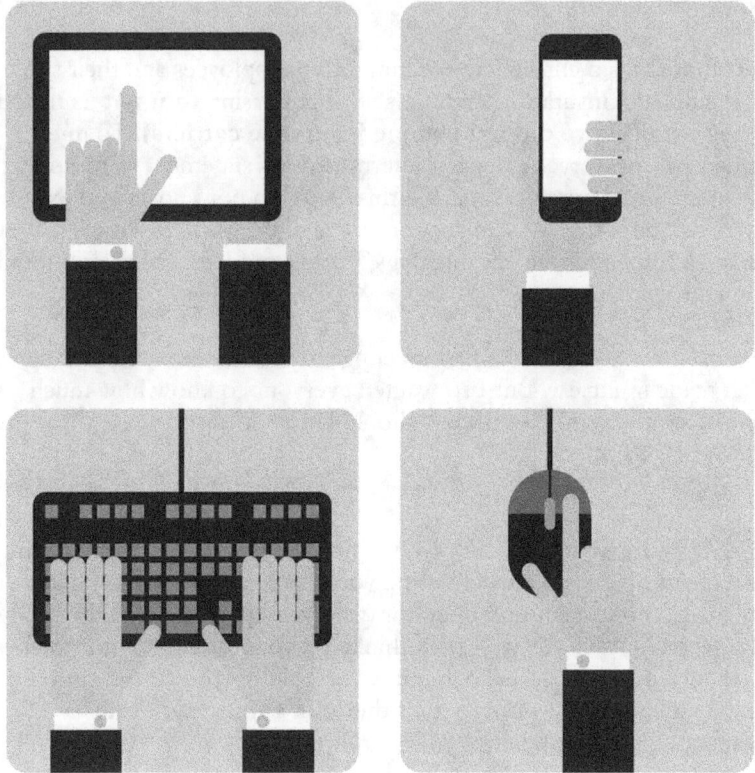

No matter the employer's size, technology plays a huge role in nearly every workplace operation. From the mailroom to the server room, technology helps workers perform their jobs quicker and with greater accuracy. In addition to their internal technology, employers often use and connect with the systems of multiple external service providers. Human resources departments rely on technology to perform much of their work.

In addition to basic computer program skills, benefit pros must master using human resource-specific systems. The human resource operation still has its share of paper processes and files; however, sophisticated Human Resource Information Systems (HRIS) use is decades old. These HRIS systems have many components (or modules) that help manage most HR functions. Also, some systems contain HR, Payroll, and Accounting modules in one, called Human Resource Management Systems (HRMS).

First Things First

Stop claiming you have good computer skills because you spend a lot of time on Facebook, Twitter, Pinterest, Instagram, and text all day. You need to be proficient in basic but often-used computer software programs. These are the minimum computer skills you need.

Must-Know Technology

Some software/technology you use in employee benefits administration is universal, like word processing, spreadsheets, publishing and presentations, and email.

I.   Word processing (e.g., Word) –

No, you won't have an assistant or secretary that writes your letters and memos; you'll have to learn how to format a proper letter and memo on your own.

• Master using templates for forms, letters, memos, brochures, newsletters, and reports
• Know how to create a letter, envelope, and label(s)
• Become a mail merge expert using mail merge data from different databases
• Master creating a table of contents, lists, columns, headers, and footers

II.   Spreadsheets (e.g., Excel) –

Don't let anyone tell you that using a spreadsheet is difficult; it's not. Spreadsheets are useful and will save you time and improve the accuracy of your work. Once you start using spreadsheets to calculate premium increases, create databases to use in merge files, or track retirement plan contributions and matches, you'll marvel at how efficient you are. You may even have to use spreadsheets as your in-house HRIS system if your company cannot afford to purchase a stand-alone system.

• Master using templates to create invoices, budgets, flow charts, and expense reports
• Master using the vertical lookup (VLOOKUP) and concatenate functions

- Learn how to create mail merge databases
- Learn how to create basic logic (if/then) statements
- Learn how to create charts and graphs

TIP: If you don't know how to access a Word or Excel template or how to start a mail merge, click on the Help menu in each application and type in *templates* or *mail merge*.

Google: How to do a mail merge in Microsoft Word or how to do a VLOOKUP in Microsoft Excel.

Search in the application: Start looking at the drop-down menu options (or use Help or Search features) until you find what you want.

III.   Presentation and Publishing (e.g., PowerPoint and Publisher) –

If you are lucky and have an eye for design, presentation, and publishing software, it will improve your benefit plan communications. First, learn the basics and then take it to the next level. Think no one uses these programs anymore; think again. PowerPoint remains as popular and boring as ever. Also, the need to create newsletters and flyers will never go out of style. Make sure you add some style to your presentations and publications. No one wants to see only text in a newsletter or flyer. Don't forget to use different fonts and font sizes too.

• Master creating presentation slides (inserting and rearranging slides, adding text, photos, charts, and graphics)

•Learn how to use an overhead projector (you shouldn't have to call the IT department each time you want to share a presentation)

• Learn how to create professional-looking newsletters, flyers, brochures, and postcards. You may not have the budget to hire an outside company. You can use an existing template to create a newsletter or design your document from scratch. (Keep a digital or paper file of examples of stylish newsletters, flyers, brochures, and postcards you like and incorporate some of their design elements. Don't, however, sacrifice content for design)

IV. Human Resource Information System (HRIS) –

HRIS systems contain much more than employee benefits data. These systems often start with the recruitment of applicants and end with the termination of employment. They include modules that manage the following HR functions:

• Applicant Tracking
• General Administration
• Benefits Administration
• Leave Administration
• Salary Administration
• Performance Management

- Training
- Self-service (at the employee and manager level)
- Reports (or Queries)

Different Modules, Same Data

Sometimes the data entered into one HR module, like hire date or annual compensation, will impact what you can enter in the Benefits Administration module. To troubleshoot any issues, you need to, at a minimum, know where the information is located in the other modules. Sometimes you can edit data in other modules, or you may have view-only access—either way, you need to be familiar with the various screens and data for every module.

There are many HRIS systems, but at their most basic, HRIS system software allows for storing, manipulating, analyzing, and retrieving data. It requires customization to "set-up" the system to meet an employer's specific needs. HRIS systems may store the following types of data:

- Personal data - (name, address, SSN, DOB, gender, marital status, email address)
- Salary data - (annual base salary, hourly rate, bonuses, severance)
- Training data - (degrees, certifications, licenses, permits, classes, seminars)
- Benefits data - (eligibility and enrollment dates and plan contribution amounts)
- Leave data - (FMLA, STD, LTD, vacation, sick, paid time off (PTO), sabbatical)

Getting To Know Your HRIS System

To operate HRIS system the right way,

• **Use** a test database to practice setting up an employee record from application to termination. You do not have to worry about messing something up in this practice environment

• **Collaborate** with other HR staff members to learn how to use the modules they use in their work. Offer to be a backup when they are out of the office or overwhelmed with work. They will be more inclined to teach you what they know if they know it may help them in the long run

• Learn how to create or query your reports from the system. Again, use the HRIS test database to practice creating your reports. You can also use existing reports and modify them for your needs

• Save your modified report with a new file name. You don't want to save over an existing report, even in a test environment. Pay attention to how colleagues created their reports so that you don't just copy or build on top of something but understand how they made the report

HRIS System With Payroll Module

We haven't talked about the relationship between Human Resources, Accounting, and Payroll, but it is significant. The payroll function relies on HR to collect and input certain information from new and existing employees to process a paycheck and perform other accounting functions. This data includes name, address, SSN, DOB, hire date, work-in-state, live-in-state, salary, federal and state tax information, and an identifying employee number.

The HR and Payroll functions must also collaborate in gathering and submitting legally mandated reports and disclosures. The data gathering and reporting includes quarterly tax reports, annual benefit plan disclosures, and other required information for federal and state agencies. Having a system that HR and Payroll can share or both have access to is ideal; however, it does not always happen.

Even though they use a lot of the same information, Human Resources and Payroll departments may decide they want to have separate IT systems for the following reasons:

• Not wanting to take the time to set up a new, shared system
• Not wanting to learn how to use a new, shared system
• Not wanting others to have access to "their" system (security and territorial issues)
• Data conversion concerns (how to get the current data into the new system)
• Performance concerns (unique contribution or calculation rules not in the new system)
• Third-party vendor and service provider concerns (the system may be incompatible)

Most HRIS/Payroll or HRMS systems can handle the information technology needs of the HR and Payroll functions and their third-party service providers. But there are things an HRIS system cannot address, including territorial, power, and trust issues between these two functions. It is unfortunate, but these "soft" issues are what prevent many companies from implementing one HRIS/Payroll system. Instead, they maintain separate systems, often created by different vendors and often requiring a third system or "fix" to allow these two systems to communicate.

Even if you are lucky enough to work in an environment with one HRIS/Payroll system, chances are you will not have access (view or edit) to the payroll side. Don't think of this as a bad thing. Limiting access to payroll processing features is important to prevent fraud, theft, or carelessness. But to make up for your lack of access, develop a good working relationship with your Payroll Administrator and the Accounting staff responsible for processing payments to insurance and other benefit plan service providers.

TIP: Benefit pros need to work with Payroll and Accounting to meet legal and administrative requirements. Unless there is a legal reason not to, never deny or delay providing Payroll the information it needs to do its job. And if there is a legal reason for not sharing, tell them.

Insurer and Third Party Administrator (TPA) Systems – These systems transmit data from your HRIS system to the insurer or service provider's system or vice versa. You should receive instructions from the insurer, TPA, or other service provider about specific system requirements to transmit and receive data. You may need to work with your HRIS department or Information Technology (IT)/Information Services (IS) department to create the files required to transmit and receive data files. On the other hand, if you do not have an HRIS system, you may have to type data into these external systems. Again, you should receive specific instructions from the insurer or TPA on accessing and using their systems.

Benefit Plan Calculators and Decision Support Systems – Benefits technology just keeps getting better. Now, in addition to employer databases that make benefit plan administration easier, there are employee-centric apps and calculators that make choosing and using a health and retirement plan easier. Benefit pros need to be up on the latest cool tools.

To start, create a list of available tools. Start with the tools your benefit plan vendors provide and add to that.

• Health Insurance Price Transparency Calculators
• Prescription Drug Cost Tools
• Retirement Savings Calculators
• Social Security Benefits Calculator
• Retirement Plan Rating Tools (e.g., BrightScope.com)
• Health Plan Recommendation Tools (e.g., HoneyInsured.com, StrideHealth.com)
• Health, Wellness, and Fitness Apps and Devices (e.g., Apple HealthKit app, Fitbit)

Post the list of tools on your intranet and send email and text updates.

You may think it's not your job to track benefit plan calculators and apps, and technically you're right. However, people will surprise you with their expectations of you as an employee benefits pro. There is an expectation that you know all things health insurance and retirement plan related. They will cut you some slack on dental, vision, life, and disability insurance, but not the health and retirement stuff.

Know More, Do More With Tech

You will use the latest technology as an employee benefits professional. Social media, websites, blogs, webcasts, and videos all have their place in today's benefits office. But it would help if you still had a solid foundation in composing, merging, and comparing documents. It would help if you also understood database management systems like Excel, HRIS, and insurer and TPA systems.

HR departments often have access to some IT support. However, the expectation is that you will use the technology available with minimum instruction. But that does not mean you should learn just enough to do your daily work. Learn as much as you can about these systems to improve your work.

For example: Say you need to send 15 COBRA election notices to recently terminated employees. What technology skills do you employ to get the job done right and fast?

• Do you type 15 separate notices using a word processing application?

• Do you create one Microsoft Word mail merge document and individually type in the names, addresses, and dates that will merge with the master document?

• Do you query a list of names, addresses, and dates from your HRIS system, save it in Excel, and format it to merge with the Word master document?

• Do you process the notices within the HRIS system's COBRA module?

TIP: Using software and other technology is more than clicking on icons and inputting data into fields. Know the "why" and "what" of the task(s), as well as what system functions take place to give you the end result you want. A few simple examples:

EX1 – HRIS systems assign new employees an ID number. This unique ID number prevents employees from being confused with others with similar names and other identifying information (it also helps if a name was misspelled when originally entered into the system).

EX2 – Entering the date of birth in an HRIS system allows that data to be used in various calculations like projected retirement date or Medicare eligibility date.

Think about how you use technology and why. Be able to explain the how and why to others. This ensures you have a good understanding of the technology. When training someone on how to use a software application, NEVER say, *I don't know why we have to do this, but I was told to do it so I'm telling you*

What To Do With What You Know

Documentation, Checklists, and Procedures – Say What!

One of the many reasons I prefer the written word to the spoken word is that people can't claim I said something I did not. Well, they can, but it is easy to disprove their claims. Why this is important as an employee benefits pro, people will say you said things you did not say. It will be uncomfortable. You will feel the need to defend yourself.

There are, however, legitimate reasons why people will try to put words in your mouth:

• They misunderstood what you said
• They sincerely thought you said something you did not
• They did not listen clearly to what you said

• They heard what they wanted to hear

Four bullets to say one thing: they have an agenda when they come to you for assistance. That does not make them bad people. They want a resolution (in their favor) to an issue. Their insurance claim was not paid in full, or they did not know they could only change plans mid-year if they experienced a qualified life event. They want their insurance claim paid in full, and they want to change plans, and you told them they could, even if you didn't.

There is no way to avoid people putting words in your mouth, including supervisors and fellow benefit pros. However, you can protect yourself from false allegations. You can document and create checklists and procedures to protect yourself and your reputation from little white lies and ensure your responses and actions are uniform.

Documentation – Make a note of conversations you have with supervisors, managers, workers, workers' family members, service providers, insurers, etc.

• Inform the other party that you will take notes

• Include the date, time, name (and work title)

• Get the facts (what, when, how, where), with as much detail as you can extract

• Ask what resolution the other party expects (if appropriate)

• Review your understanding of the issue with the other party, ask for further clarification, and request an agreement

• Write down anything else that will remind you of the conversation (e.g., was the person ill that day, or did they just return from vacation). Don't describe people in a way you wouldn't want to be revealed (e.g., the fat, black lady from Accounting)

You can place these notes in a file you have for that individual or company (scan them into a digital file or place them in a paper file). Or, you can shred the notes after the issue is resolved.

I recommend filing notes on complex or ongoing issues like medical leaves of absence and shredding the small stuff like routine claims that are resolved. HR departments often keep separate benefits files. You should have a separate file for every third party you work with to administer your benefits program and a general benefits file. Don't create a file with your supervisor and co-workers' names on them.

Importance of Checklists and Procedures

There's a lot to learn about employee benefits, but memorizing it all is not a good strategy. Therefore, you need to create lists and procedures. Not only will creating checklists and procedures improve your work accuracy and efficiency, but you can also use this information to train new and current benefits staff. It may sound silly or unnecessary, but I like creating lists and procedures for every benefits task. And the more detailed and exhaustive the lists and procedures you make, the better.

Checklists and Procedures:

For me, checklists and procedures go together. You can create the procedure and then the checklist or vice versa. Both the checklist and the procedure should include every step and every detail required to complete the task. Include visuals for every procedure and use numbered and bulleted lists.

•Create a summary statement that describes the procedure (e.g., This is a procedure for enrolling or re-enrolling new/rehires in the company's medical, dental, vision, life, and retirement plans)

• Write down every step required to perform the task (e.g., open up the HRIS application, click on the benefits administration module icon, select the new enrollment box, click on the employee number drop-down box to find the employee, confirm name... Write Down Everything In The Form of Numbers or Bulleted Steps)

• Include computer screenshots and highlight each action (e.g., if your procedure refers to a drop-down box, include a screenshot of the box and highlight the area). Don't know how to take a screenshot in a particular application? Read the application notes, ask an IT professional or Google—How to take a screenshot in (blank) application

• Include samples of documents and forms with an explanation of all the information included — (e.g., enrollment forms, government reports)

• Reference any employer policies related to the procedure (e.g., handling benefits deductions when workers are on an 'approved' medical leave of absence)

• Include any contact information of the person to call if there are issues with the task (name, email, phone number, etc.). For example, if there will be a delay in remitting retirement plan contributions because of an internal system issue, call the record keeper

What To Write Procedures For...

Write and organize procedures in the order that they are likely to occur. For example, if employees may enroll in the health plan when first hired but must wait 30 days to enroll in the retirement plan, write the health plan enrollment procedure first.

• How To Enroll Employees In Benefit Plans (Internal and External System Procedures)
• Accessing Third Party Vendor Systems
• How To Make Plan Enrollment Changes
• Running (Querying) HRIS System Reports
• How To Pay Premium Statements (Insurance Bills)
• How To Remit Employee Retirement Plan Contributions
• How To Track Medical Leaves of Absence (FMLA, STD, ADA)
• How To Bill Employees For Unpaid Benefit Plan Payments
• Preparing For Plan Audits
• Preparing Employee Benefits Annual Returns (Form 5500)
• Preparing For Nondiscrimination Testing
• Preparing For Plan Renewal, And Open Enrollment
• Processing Retirement Plan Withdrawal and Loan Applications
• How To Terminate Benefit Plan Coverage
• Preparing/Sending COBRA notices

What To Write Checklists For...

Checklists do not need to be complicated. Choose a checklist template from Microsoft Word or some other application and modify it for your needs. The primary purpose of the list is to ensure consistency of action and response.

• Every Employee Benefits Procedure
• Employee Benefits Packet
• New Hire Orientation
• Live Event Processes
• Plan Billing (Premium Statement) Audits
• Plan Reporting Requirements And Deadlines
• Address And Name Changes
• Training
• Exit Interviews

Sample Checklist (assisting employees that have a critical illness):

• Add information to Leave of Absence log
• Activate paid and unpaid leave programs
• Assist with the completion of short- and long-term disability applications
• Help apply for Social Security disability insurance, if applicable
• Investigate state assistance programs for health care, mortgage, and utilities
• Investigate public assistance programs that provide transportation and food delivery
• Activate Employee Assistance Program benefits for employee and their dependents
• Provide pension plan benefits projections or account balance information
• Verify life insurance benefits
• Ensure completion of life insurance and retirement plan beneficiary forms
• Offer to meet with a spouse or significant other to answer any questions
• Provide health insurance claim assistance

TIP Print your procedures and checklists and place them in a binder. That's your Employee Benefits Procedure Manual.

I don't mind having a Word or PDF version of procedures, but I must have a hardcopy version also. I like writing notes in the margins that I update a few times per year in digital format. I mean, what's an office without at least one binder, even in the digital age?

Interpersonal Relationships At Work – I Like And Respect You

Is any topic more popular in the business world than interpersonal relationships in the workplace? I don't think so. Instruction on how to understand yourself and others, deal with "Jerks at Work" (an actual book title), and "tips" articles abound. Here are just a few titles:

Books:
- *Emotional Intelligence*
- *How To Win Friends and Influence People*
- *Men Are From Mars, Women Are From Venus*
- *Coping With Difficult People*
- *Verbal Judo, The Gentle Art of Persuasion*
- *Disarming the Narcissist: Surviving And Thriving With The Self-Absorbed*

Articles:
- *8 Tips for Developing Positive Relationships*
- *13 Options to Improve Your Work Relationships*
- *6 Bomb Proof Workplace Relationship Skills…*
- *13 Workplace Relationship Tips*

- *How to Improve Interpersonal Relationships at Work…*
- *Managing Relationships*

These titles can give the impression that the workplace is a battlefield. But not all workplace relationships are difficult. Some are pleasant, productive, and cooperative from the start. However, writing about problem-free workplace relationships isn't informative, so we are stuck with *Jerks At Work*. I love that title!

Feel free to read some of these publications—some of the books listed above are classics. And, as a benefits pro, you will get a lot of practice navigating interpersonal workplace relationships. Here are the players and how they are likely to interact with you:

Third-Party Vendors and Service Providers –

Some of the best work relationships benefit pros have are with third-party vendors and service providers. Third-party vendors and service providers include all of the specialized services Benefits departments employ to help manage their benefits programs and keep them compliant, such as:

actuaries, retirement plan record keepers, financial advisors, lawyers, brokers, and insurance and wellness company representatives

These professionals help you establish and manage your benefits programs. They may help you design the plan, addressing issues such as who is eligible to enroll and when. They may also assist with federal and state plan compliance, communication, and problem resolution.

To get the most out of third-party vendor and service provider work relationships:

• Learn as much as you can about your vendor's organization, where it ranks in the industry and its viability—no one wants to rely on a vendor that has financial problems and may not be in business long

• Know your vendor representatives – ask about their work and educational background as it relates to the services they will be providing you

• Get to know the people behind the scenes – visit the claims processing, call center, or administrative offices of the service provider

• Communicate with your providers – don't just contact a provider when there is an issue to resolve. Stay in contact by asking questions and sharing ideas or concerns about the latest trends and compliance issues in the industry. But don't overdo it

• Thank your service providers for their help—show respect for the help and expertise providers bring to the table

Third-party vendors and service providers can be a great source of information and you can learn a lot from these specialists. But like all relationships, things can get rocky from time to time.

-Choosing the wrong vendor or service provider – choosing a vendor because of price or geographical convenience instead of the ability to meet the needs of the plan

-Ignoring the advice of a vendor or service provider – you don't have to agree with everything your service provider says, but you should at least evaluate their advice

-Overestimating the advice of a vendor or service provider – never accept every word of advice from a service provider just because you think they know more about a subject than you. Do your own research and ask questions…

TIP: You are responsible for learning as much as possible about the benefit plans you administer and insurance and retirement plans in general. You cannot rely solely on service providers to teach you everything you need to know. They will respect you more if they know you want to meet them halfway. Also, they will be less inclined to try to talk over your head or provide glib answers to your questions. Relationships are a two-way street.

Employers have a legal responsibility to design and administer their benefits program for the benefit of employees. Even if a vendor or service provider agrees to assume some of that responsibility, they can't and won't assume it all. Benefit pros must work with third-party vendors but not follow their advice without question.

Workplace Colleagues –

Third-party vendors and service providers are people you work with occasionally. You don't have to see or talk to them every day like you do your workplace colleagues. Some work colleagues you interact with more than others; however, it is not the frequency of interaction or the person's proximity that determines if a workplace interpersonal relationship will be a challenge; it's the people involved. Benefit pros team up regularly with:

• Human Resource (HR) personnel
• Finance personnel
• IT personnel
• Marketing, Safety, Fitness and Wellness
• Employees

HR: (generalists, recruiters, trainers, compensation and benefit pros) – Collaborate on recruiting, new hire orientations, employee and supervisor training, performance issues related to leave of absence or medical issues, compensation and severance package analysis and layoffs

Finance: (accounting, payroll, auditing) – Collaborate on evaluating benefit plan vendor contracts and fees, processing vendor bills, deducting and remitting employee and employer payments, preparing tax and other financial forms, and auditing benefit plans

IT: (developers, email administrators, trainers) – Collaborate on setting up, maintaining, and troubleshooting systems and programs that support HR functions. Help with company-wide digital communications like intranet, email, and text messages

Marketing: Collaborate on developing or evaluating branded information

Safety, Fitness and Wellness: Collaborate on organizing flu shots, wellness screenings, CPR and first aid training; benefits, health, and wellness fairs; health and fitness promotions; workplace violence prevention, and other safety training

Employees: You need to be a people person to work as an employee benefit professional. Not. It helps if you like or don't dislike interacting with employees, but being an extrovert or someone who thrives on personal interaction is not essential to being a top benefits pro. Knowledge is key to employee benefits, and so is flexibility and respect.

"The less said about this one, the better."

Think about it. Employees contact benefit pros when they need assistance with sensitive and emotional issues, including dealing with death, chronic illness, drug abuse, and financial hardship. They aren't always polite when they ask for help, and some are downright vicious. Below are just a few of my most challenging moments working with employees. I didn't take them personally, but I did feel the sting of some of them. I also learned a lot about how people can act when they experience stress and anxiety.

• I received an email from one employee saying, "You must think we're all stupid..."

• On my first day at a new job (open enrollment had just ended, but people were still submitting their plan elections), a senior manager called me and said, "Let me speak to someone who *actually* makes decisions; I'm sure that's not you..."

• I once had a manager scream so loud at me over the phone that I could not understand a word she said. It was late on a Friday afternoon, and she needed to see her psychiatrist but could not afford the visit. She had exhausted the health plan's paid mental health visits for the year

• Oh, and one time this highly compensated employee cried in my office and told me I was ruining her life because of a flexible spending account misunderstanding involving a small amount of money

I'm No Social Worker

Working in employee benefits can feel like being a social worker. In fact, benefit pros assume the role of a social worker more often than you might think. Your broad knowledge of federal, state, and local social programs is handy in these unusual situations. Knowledge of government and nonprofit health and financial services programs and benefits like Social Security, Medicare, and Children's Health Insurance Programs (CHIP) sets you apart from other benefit pros. It also allows you to help many employees and their families access benefits that complement or supplement the workplace benefits program.

I've introduced and helped many low-wage, single parents apply for free health insurance for their children. Access to government-subsidized insurance meant they paid the individual health insurance premium instead of the more costly and unaffordable family plan premium. There were also times when, after reading about a nonprofit's new government program or service, I helped workers apply for disability or mental health benefits for family members. I've helped people apply for Medicare, Social Security, government disability benefits, and numerous other social programs.

You don't have to be an expert on Social Security, Medicare, CHIP, wills, trusts, or health orders to help employees with health and retirement matters. You can, however, provide basic information and refer employees to professional help. You can also keep a supply of program brochures, which you can usually get for free or a small fee.

The 99% (of Employee Benefit Issues)

Most employees who come to you for assistance will be pleasant and have easy-to-address issues. And the ones who aren't attacking you personally. It's only natural for employees to feel some apprehension when it comes to issues they encounter with their benefit plans. Benefit plans cost a lot of money and can be confusing. Therefore, employees feel out of their comfort zone, and sometimes their behavior reflects their discomfort.

Most of your employee encounters will be about medical claims and leaves of absence. These issues may seem minor, but they are important to employees needing your help. My philosophy on addressing employee benefits issues, big or small, is to give them what they want whenever possible. I can't tell you how many times I've said the following, in one way or another:

I am looking for a way to say yes to your request. To give you what you want. I don't want you to be unhappy or in distress. If I can find a way to resolve this issue in your favor, I will. If I can't, I will tell you exactly why.

The Good, The Bad And The Worst Workplace Relationships

What makes some workplace colleagues difficult to work with? For me the most difficult people to work with have several of these qualities:

• Dishonest
• Insincere
• Jealous
• Manipulative
• Mean
• Non-collaborative
• Resistant to change
• Vengeful

Confession: I once had a benefits colleague with a special nickname for me that she willingly shared with everyone. And she tried to undermine me at every turn and was very successful (I quit). My relationship with her was the worst example of a workplace interpersonal relationship that no expert could help. But the many wonderful workplace relationships I had more than made up for the toxic one I had with her and other "challenging" colleagues. Some of my greatest workplace relationships were with individuals whose work I supervised and others I teamed up with to work on specific projects.

The Supervisor

Like most people, I've had good and bad supervisors. I think I'm batting 500 in this regard. For me, a good supervisor is someone:

• Who has my best interest at heart
• Who cares about my development but also sees me as a human being
• Who doesn't talk negatively behind my back, especially with staff in the department
• Who doesn't lose control of his or her emotions
• Who has self-confidence and does not need their ego stroked
• Who shares
• Who has the knowledge and seeks more

Yeah, the knowledge thing means less to me than the personality thing. I'm not perfect, but I can't imagine yelling, losing my cool, or trying to undermine someone I supervise. You can learn a lot from a good and lousy supervisor. The best supervisors are those that ask, "what do you need or want and how can I help?"

Me, The Supervisor

I was initially a reluctant supervisor. I preferred performing technical tasks to interacting with people. However, I came to enjoy collaborating with and instructing other benefit pros. I saw it as challenging my character, temperament, and intellect. How do I treat people who rely on me to train and nurture them? How patient am I with an assistant struggling to understand a concept? How quickly do I become frustrated, and how do I express my frustration? How knowledgeable am I, and do I have anything to offer?

My philosophy about supervising staff mirrors my philosophy on life— learn and learn some more. I want everyone around me to know what I know, and I want to know what they know. So many supervisors hold back their knowledge and are reluctant to answer questions because of their insecurities. Some are not good at explaining anything, but look out for those who can but won't.

TIP: Read the books and articles on managing workplace interpersonal relationships if you want. As much as I like to read, these publications never really did it for me. They make me doubt myself more than anything else. **What works for me when dealing with "Jerks At Work" is to avoid them and focus on my positive relationships with others**. And sometimes, you just have to move on.

Upping Your Game and Enhancing Your Credibility

Due to the sensitive nature of some benefits information and the financial stakes of many benefits decisions, benefit pros must work hard to gain credibility. Being knowledgeable about your organization's benefits program represents just one notch on your credibility belt. To add a few more notches, you will need to go above and beyond the requirements in your job description. That means being able to assist in all matters of health and welfare insurance and retirement planning. For example, helping employees understand and apply for benefits outside the workplace.

You Need To Know Something About Medicare And Social Security (SS)...

Many employee benefits professionals working in the private sector know little about the federal Medicare and Social Security (SS) programs. Lack of knowledge about government benefits is true of pros in the public and not-for-profit sectors too. And that's unfortunate because employees have a lot of questions about both programs. They see (tax) deductions from their pay for these programs and assume HR can answer their Medicare and SS questions.

Of course, it is not your job to counsel employees on their Medicare and SS options, but why not help provide a basic understanding of the programs? If the concern is legal liability, don't give advice. If the problem is fear of providing the wrong information, ensure you know what you are talking about before opening your mouth, and always include a verbal or written disclaimer. And if the concern is that Medicare and SS benefits are not your areas of expertise, study up.

Medicare 101 For Benefit Pros

Benefit pros don't need to know everything about Medicare, but you should have a good understanding of these five (5) basic Medicare features.

-Who is eligible to receive Medicare benefits and when—U. S. citizens or permanent residents aged 65 and over, young people with disabilities, and those with end-stage renal disease. In general, eligibility requires paying Medicare (FICA) taxes for 40 quarters (ten years)

-How and when to apply for Medicare—Individuals who are age 65 AND receiving a Social Security check are automatically enrolled in Medicare and will receive a Medicare card in the mail. If they are not receiving a SS check, they must contact the Social Security office (yes SS handles Medicare so they are called SS offices) to enroll

-What to do about Medicare if an employee is age 65, works full-time, and is enrolled in their employer's health plan—Enroll in Medicare Part A when first eligible. He or she can delay enrolling in Medicare Parts B and D. Contact SS to enroll in Medicare Part A and discuss delaying enrollment in Parts B and D

-What are the different (main) parts of Medicare and what do they cover—The Medicare program consists of four main parts:

Part A (primarily covers hospital (inpatient) care)

Part B (primarily covers physician services (outpatient care))

Part C or Medicare Advantage (private health insurance elected in lieu of Parts A and B)

Part D (standalone prescription drug program for individuals enrolled in Medicare Parts A and B or enrolled in a Medicare Advantage plan that does not have prescription drug coverage)

-What are Medicare Supplement plans and how do they work – Individuals who enroll in Medicare Parts A and B (aka original or traditional Medicare) can purchase a Medicare supplement plan to cover expenses not paid by Parts A and B. Individuals enrolled in Medicare Advantage plans cannot purchase a Medicare supplement plan

Another Medicare issue that comes up involves individuals who are eligible to enroll in both Medicare and the employer health plan. Technically, these individuals can delay signing up for Medicare if they are enrolled in an employer-sponsored plan. However, because it cost nothing to enroll in Medicare Part A, most working, Medicare-eligible workers enroll. Unlike Medicare Part A, Part B does have a monthly premium and enrollment is often delayed.

These workers will have questions about Medicare and workplace health coverage eligibility. They may also question which plan pays what when they receive medical care. The Centers for Medicare and Medicaid Services provides a free online guide: *"Medicare & Other Health Benefits: Your Guide To Who Pays First."* Benefit pros should read this guide and its updates. It is also an excellent resource to provide to employees and not just Medicare-eligible employees. Many employees help their parents or disabled loved ones with health care issues and would benefit from the guide.

Confession: I've lost count of how many times I received angry complaints from employees who did not enroll in a workplace health plan but thought the company was taking a deduction for the plan from their pay anyway. **They confused the Medicare tax (usually coded as HI for health insurance) with employer private health insurance coverage**. Even though the "deduction" is listed under the "Tax" header of their paycheck…

I'm not trying to make fun of anyone, but I was surprised and confused the first time it happened. After it happened a few more times, I modified a pay stub in Adobe (actually, it was a check advice) and explained the various taxes and deductions. I included a note about the Medicare tax being a tax, not a health insurance deduction. The department included sample check advices in all new hire benefits packets, reviewed during benefits orientations, and included on the company intranet.

Social Security (SS) 101 For Benefit Pros

Unlike Medicare, employees feel slightly more confident about how the Social Security (SS) retirement program works and when to apply for benefits. The reality is many workers know very little about the SS program. For example, a significant number think that the SS taxes they pay fund their specific benefits. And many do not know their SS full retirement age and that they receive a smaller benefit amount when they elect to receive benefits before normal retirement. Or that they can receive significantly higher monthly benefits if they delay receiving benefits up to age 70.

Employers play a significant role in financing SS benefits. It is in their best interest to help workers get the maximum SS benefits so they retire when they want, not when they can.

The federal Social Security program is complicated. There are SS experts with decades of experience that don't know everything there is to know about SS. No one expects benefit pros to know as much as an SS expert dedicated to the field, but the top benefit pros will completely understand these five basic SS features.

-Who is eligible to receive SS benefits and when—SS provides cash benefits to retirees, widows/widowers, and disabled individuals who are unable to work. In general, eligibility requires paying SS (OASDI) taxes for 40 quarters (ten years). Not all jobs require workers to pay SS taxes (for example, not all state and local government and teaching jobs pay SS taxes)

-How and when to apply for SS—Individuals can apply for SS benefits online or in person at their local SS office

When to start receiving benefits is an individual's most important SS decision. Workers can start receiving SS retirement benefits as early as age 62. They will receive reduced benefits forever due to the early election of benefits. Workers receive full benefits if they wait until full retirement age. Full retirement age depends on the year born, and for most current workers is between and including age 66 to age 67. Individuals can delay receipt of SS benefits up to age 70 and receive additional benefits of 8% per year for each year after full retirement age up to age 70

-How to estimate Social Security benefits amounts. The Social Security Administration (SSA) mails annual benefits estimates to workers aged 60 and over. Younger workers can use the SSA online benefits estimator tool:
(file://localhost/ (https/::secure.ssa.gov:acu:ACU_KBA:main.jsp%3FURL=:apps8 z:ARPI:main.jsp%3Flocale=en&LVL=4) to project their future benefits

-How Social Security works when still receiving a paycheck. Employees can collect SS benefits while still working. However, there is a reduction in benefits if the employee is not at least full-retirement age AND earning income above a certain level

-What things should employees consider to receive the maximum SS benefits—Workers should maintain consistent yet increasing earnings. Also, they should coordinate their decision to collect SS benefits with spouses. Lastly, workers should try to delay receiving benefits until age 70, if possible

How Much Help To Provide With Medicare and Social Security Issues

Benefit pros can decide how much detailed information they want to provide about Medicare. Employees will ask questions and greatly desire your guidance, so why not give it to them? Be careful of the information you provide, and always recommend that they speak with a Medicare counselor regarding their specific situation.

For Social Security (SS), workers need help estimating benefits and deciding when to receive them. Provide some basic education about SS retirement benefits. Point workers towards online tools that allow them to estimate their SS benefits at different ages. In addition, let them know that some firms specialize in providing SS advisory services to help employees determine the optimal time to start receiving benefits.

Consider creating a one-page guide that includes Medicare and Social Security information, important dates, and contact information.

You Need To Know How To Assist All Workers...

HR people know the company's business hierarchy better than most other professionals. Unfortunately, they often consciously or unconsciously treat some workers better than others. They respond to their inquiries quicker, with more detail, patience, and energy. Now, there is nothing wrong with a quick and thorough response, but benefit pros need to bring this same energy to every employee encounter. It's not about treating everyone equally so that you seem fair; it's about being a reliable resource and problem solver for everyone you serve.

Your employee benefits-related encounters with employees at the top of the business hierarchy differ from those at the middle and lower tiers. Top-level employees will typically contact the head of your department or division with a benefit plan issue, which will then be pushed down to you—sometimes with a reminder of how important this person is and how, when, and to whom to respond. These managers may not know who you are but will know the head of your division. It's also not uncommon to receive benefits inquiries from a top-level employee's spouse. These messages may or may not be sent directly to you. Meanwhile, mid to lower-level employees will typically contact you directly for assistance.

It may not be possible for benefit pros to ignore the business hierarchy completely. You may indeed put in a little more effort to help the CEO's wife with her health insurance claim than you would with the janitor trying to find a new doctor. But trust me when I tell you that you will learn more about your capabilities as an employee benefits pro when you help workers with the least amount of health insurance or retirement savings knowledge.

Confession: I once worked with an employee who was in his mid-40s and never had private insurance. He never paid an insurance premium, deductible, or coinsurance and needed help understanding these terms and how they worked. He was a health care receiver, never a payer. My challenge was to explain a concept (insurance) to someone who had never had any insurance (homeowners, auto, life, or health).

Don't Explain, Do
Ten minutes into my first meeting with this employee, I felt challenged to come up with an entirely new way of explaining health insurance. The conversation vastly differed from my conversations with new health plan enrollees. I never once thought that someone would not know how to take the first step in using insurance coverage.

So, this is what I did:
I asked the employee if his wife could join our conversation, and with his consent, I called her. She informed me that she went to the free clinic and showed them her new ID card that our plan issued and was told that she would not be treated. I told her that was correct because the private insurance her husband purchased through the company replaced the free,

public care they once received. I told them that the care they once received at no cost would now mean money out of their pockets, in addition to what we subtracted from his paycheck. I also told them that based on his income, they were not eligible for Medicaid but that their son could get free health coverage under the state Children's Health Insurance Program (CHIP). I printed a CHIP application, and we filled it out in my office. I told the employee to give it to his wife to sign and mail. I also gave them a stamped envelope with the address of the CHIP office. The next thing I did was help him and his wife find a doctor near their home and schedule an appointment. Lastly, I found a state-based premium support program they could enroll in that would help them pay part of the medical plan premiums. These programs help the working poor afford health insurance. I helped them complete and submit the application.

How was I able to do this? I did a lot of research and learned about these programs early in my career.

This situation with this particular employee changed the way I approached my job. It made me even more research-focused, looking beyond the benefits the firm offered. It gave me a broader view. And when I think about the Affordable Care Act bringing a lot more *Never Hads* to the private health insurance table, I am concerned about the quality of their introduction to this new world. There are many employees and families like the one I helped. Benefit professionals should learn how to meet the needs of people who have yet to receive medical care, have never had private health insurance, or come from a country that does not have private health insurance.

Learning to help all workers navigate the confusing world of employee benefits in creative ways will do a lot for your credibility. Word will get out about your willingness to assist with dignity. More workers will feel confident in tapping you as a resource and present you with even more challenges. One of my favorite benefits inquiry challenges is answering "have you heard about" questions.

Answering "Have You Heard About" Questions

As a benefits pro, you should get used to answering a lot of questions. Every day your knowledge of your organization's benefits programs as well as health, life, and disability insurance and retirement plans in general will be tested. Your ability to answer questions correctly and quickly will determine your reputation with employees and management.

The Difference Between Employee and Employer Questions

In general, individual employee benefits questions are more "me-centric," and top management questions are more global or "we-centric." An employee may ask if the plan covers a particular medical service. Top management may ask about the cost to the company to cover a specific benefit.

But one question that comes up from time to time by both groups is the "Have you heard about…" question. Sometimes this question is accompanied by a copy of a newspaper or magazine article or a link to a website. Other times there is no particular reference, just a question. And the more you can answer "yes" to the "have you heard about" questions, the better your credibility.

Responding to "Have You Heard About…" Questions

You cannot be an expert in all areas of employee benefits, but you do want to have a broad knowledge of the field. Take every opportunity to learn and be prepared to answer question outside of your day-to-day responsibilities. The less you have to say, "so and so takes care of that, I only work with (fill in the blank)," the better. Also, so and so may not always be available to help answer questions. This is your time to shine and enhance your credibility.

Assuming you are staying on top of employee benefits trends and legislation, consider creating a procedure for dealing with "have you heard about" questions.

• **Treat** all "have you heard about" questions with respect. It does not matter if the question comes from a low-level employee or top management; give it the same level of consideration. Every "have you heard about" question is an opportunity to learn or share your knowledge. Be grateful for the opportunity.

• **Anticipate** questions and prepare a response. If you stay on top of employee benefits trends, you can probably anticipate most of the questions you will get. If you do your research, you can prepare your responses in advance. People will know that you are staying on top of the latest news and laws and thinking about how it may impact the company's benefits program.

• **Ask Your Own "Have You Heard About" Questions**. Who said that you had to wait for someone else to ask questions? Ask your own questions (of your supervisor or top management). One way to do this is to prepare a short write-up about why this issue is important and your proposal for addressing or implementing it. When asking your own "have you heard about" questions, make sure you have an expert command of the information. Anticipate all follow-up questions.

It goes without saying that you should stay on top of employee benefits trends and legislation. It also goes without saying that employees will ask what you know about the latest insurance and retirement plan issues. Be prepared to answer and ask your own "have you heard about" questions. Your ability to answer these questions with confidence and authority is what makes you a *Benefits Know It All*.

Keep It To Yourself (KITY)

I'm passionate about privacy when it comes to employee benefits matters. Long before the Health Insurance Portability and Accountability Act (HIPAA) mandated privacy in health insurance matters, my philosophy was to keep all employee conversations and documents confidential. An employee has cancer; not for me to share. Employees need to borrow from their retirement plan; that's no one's business. An employee needs help with an addiction; it's simply a leave of absence issue.

Benefit pros must know and understand laws addressing the privacy of benefit plan information, including HIPAA and GINA. It is also important to participate in developing policies and procedures for safeguarding this information, especially electronic information. That means collaborating with HRIS and IT/IS professionals to make sure access to data is limited and mechanisms are in place to identify data breaches.

Sure. But the reality is benefit pros routinely violate privacy laws and regulations for several reasons.

- You have a general understanding of health care privacy laws
- You don't have a Health Information Procedures Manual
- You don't receive regular training or legal updates
- You use internal IT/IS systems that are not in full compliance with these laws
- You don't request a signed release when assisting with an insurance claim issue
- You leave private information out in the open for anyone to view
- You don't lock up your files

Or maybe it is some other reason, like... You Talk Too Much Benefits Pro.

Some benefit pros obsess over keeping employee health information private. Guilty! With these pros, employees can feel safe sharing information about their cancer treatment or their son's drug addiction. But other pros are not as respectful or discreet when handling this information.

How To Minimize Your Own Security Breaches

Employees will often provide more private health information than they need to when seeking assistance. It is your responsibility to make clear the information you do and do not need as part of the process. However, if the employee decides to share information with anyone willing to listen, that doesn't mean you can. You can't, so don't. Besides, nothing bolsters personal and professional credibility like discretion. A gossipy employee benefits pro has zero credibility.

Conversely, some benefit pros will request more private health information than they need to do their job. Sometimes these pros can over/under-empathize with an employee, viewing them as friends or foes, not clients.

Let's talk about this empathy-friend or foe thing for a second: It is sad that employees or their family members who experience a health issue are treated differently based on how well-liked that employee is by their supervisor. I know this sounds crazy, but time and time again, I witnessed supervisors trying to deny medical leave when they did not personally like an employee and offer more than is required by law to those they did. HR and other benefits staff quickly pick up their feelings and treat the employee accordingly, including how much private health information they must provide and how it is handled.

Now back to how not to violate health information privacy and security…

• Do focus on the issue
• Do handle information respectfully
• Do get written permission to release health information
• Do get written permission to assist with medical claim disputes
• Don't request information unless you need it to perform your job
• Don't share health information with any third parties unless needed to do the job
• Don't be a jerk

Federal and state laws exist to protect the privacy and security of an individual's personal health information. Unfortunately, some employee benefit pros fail to understand the breadth of these laws and unknowingly violate them. The top two things benefit pros can do to keep in compliance with health information privacy and security laws is:

1) request only the information they need to do their job and
2) not talk so much

Still, it's not easy, not sharing. Supervisors, including your own, will try to pry information out of you. Especially, if the benefits issue involves a leave of absence.

Leave Management – The Toughest Employee Benefits Function

"Nice and simple. The way a family leave policy should be."

Many of us will need to take an extended medical or personal leave of absence at some point in our work lives. Medical leaves of absence include taking time off to give birth and to receive treatment for or recover from an illness or injury. Personal leave may entail taking time off to care for or support an ill or injured family member.

Federal and state laws, employer policies, and programs allow employees to take time off from work for these absences without fear of losing their job. Benefit professionals must be aware of these laws to administer their leave programs properly. In addition, they need to stay apprised of related case law decisions to understand how the courts interpret challenges to leave policies and laws. And benefit pros need to communicate these laws, policies, and programs to employees and supervisors.

Top Challenges of Leave Management

All of this sounds straightforward, but it is not. In fact, leave administration was always my least favorite function to perform for several reasons.

• **The laws are complex**, interconnected, and overlapping. For example, an employee may have a leave situation that involves the federal or state Family and Medical Leave Act (FMLA), Americans With Disabilities Act (ADA) and Workers' Compensation (WC), or FMLA, ADA, and a short- or long-term disability policy

• **The leave situations are not always clear** and require some investigating to figure out

• **Employees may delay answering questions** and completing paperwork to justify and document the leave

• **Supervisors may express exasperation and hostility**. Often questioning the legitimacy of the need for leave and its duration

• **Electronic leave management systems** available to track leave don't always work in the real world. You need a system that is compatible with your HR and Payroll systems and takes into consideration the various federal and state laws and company policies

My greatest challenge with leave management/administration is working with supervisors and, to a lesser extent, employees. Working with an insensitive supervisor or an entitled employee makes leave management more like babysitting. It is incredible how something as important as taking time off for your health or caring for a loved one can turn the workplace into a battleground.

I once heard a supervisor say that she was not surprised that an employee who had a heart attack would take 12 weeks of FMLA leave because he was always a problem employee. Pretty cold. But employees can be equally insensitive to the needs of their employer. Often mistakenly believing that their need for medical or personal leave entitles them to do whatever they want. I once worked with an employee diagnosed with cancer who would leave work whenever she disagreed with her supervisor. She claimed the stress made her feel ill.

Conquering Leave Management Challenges

Leave management is more about managing the feelings and actions of supervisors and employees than anything else. To have a successful leave management system, you must be highly knowledgeable about related federal and state leave legislation, case law, and your company's leave policies. Your knowledge will protect your organization from discrimination claims while assisting employees in getting the time off they are entitled to. It will also help you manage the battles between supervisors and employees.

• To learn more about FMLA, log onto the DOL website - http://www.dol.gov/whd/fmla/

• To learn about state leave laws, log onto the state government website where the employee works (for example, the District of Columbia has its own FMLA leave law and California has a personal family leave law as well)

• To learn more about ADA, log onto the DOJ website - http://www.ada.gov

• To learn more about workers' compensation, log onto the DOL website for a list of each state's WC website - http://www.dol.gov/owcp/dfec/regs/compliance/wc.htm

• Learn everything about the short- and long-term disability policies your organization offers by reading all plan documentation (don't just focus on how employees apply for coverage, know what benefits are available and excluded and why)

• Create an Excel leave tracking system or purchase a standalone leave management system. Your Human Resources Management (Information) System (HRMS/HRIS) may already include a forgotten leave module

• Maintain detailed documentation (eligibility, approval, dates, insurance payments, retirement plan participation, telephone conversations, emails, and any additional notes about the leave)

• Don't forget privacy (supervisors and managers don't need to know everything about a leave request; just that their employee is eligible for leave and the expected leave duration)

A few more thoughts on leave management.

Leave management is tricky. That is why it is important to be cautious when talking to an employee or supervisor about a leave of absence.

• Your statements may be interpreted as support or approval

• Employees may try to get you to commit to allowing them more time off than they are entitled to

• Supervisors may try to bully you into getting the person back to work sooner than they are ready or are legally obligated to, or

• Management may want you to discourage the worker from returning

My advice on leave management: don't do or say anything that may come back to haunt you.

Confession: This confession involves someone else's lousy judgment this time, not my own. This one is a real doozy.

An HR Manager once left a voicemail informing an employee on a permitted 12-month medical leave of absence that the firm was terminating her employment and that she would shortly receive a termination of employment letter. The employee was distraught when she called to tell me she intended to return to work before her leave expired in one week.

TIP: Never use voicemail to terminate someone's employment. It's not a courtesy call; it's cruel. Don't assume that a person will not return from an extended leave of absence—it happens. Wait until the leave expires before acting.

I bet you want to know what happened with the employee and the HR Manager. The employee returned to work for a very short time before resigning for health reasons and the HR Manager was promoted. True story.

Finding Your Place In The HR Department

Would I have received a promotion if I had tried to terminate an employee's employment prematurely? No. Would my credibility have taken a hit inside and outside the HR department? Yes. Benefit pros can't get away with making mistakes their HR colleagues just brush off. We don't always have the same level of support within HR as the other functions do.

Benefit professionals can sometimes feel like the stepchildren of the HR department. They are often losing the spotlight to their more "outgoing" colleagues. You know, the recruiters, generalists, trainers, and employee relations folks. While we work behind the scenes to ensure our benefit plans comply with tax laws and other regulations, the other HR staff are chatting it up all day. We poke out our heads once a year to host the annual open enrollment; they host monthly supervisor training. Are they nicer than us? Do employees like them more than us? Are they more needed than us? No. No. And, No.

There are many reasons why benefit professionals are often anonymous at work. Sometimes their anonymity is self-imposed, but other times HR upper management shoves them in this direction.

Three (3) Reasons for Self-Imposed Anonymity

• More comfortable dealing with technical issues than people. (Most pros I know enjoy the technical and people aspects of the job)

• Fear of being bombarded with questions. (Oddly, some benefit pros think that employees should just read the benefit plan material and understand them as a pro would)

• Think their job is to wait for someone to ask them a question. (It's not entirely their fault as new pros are never encouraged or taught to offer help in advance of a problem)

Three (3) Reasons "Others" Keep Benefits in the Back Room

• HR department leaders may have a preconceived notion about the personality of benefit pros and, therefore, consciously or unconsciously limit their interaction with employees

• HR department leaders may have a limited understanding of benefits and prefer not to have too many discussions about them lest someone else find out their ignorance

• HR department leaders may simply find benefits boring and assume that all other employees do too

It's Time to Show Them What You Got

Benefit pros, who focus most of their time on the behind-the-scenes stuff, are hurting their career. Have you ever heard of out of sight, out of mind? So, knowing you are not one of the cool kids in the department, what's an employee benefits pro to do to get some attention? The most important thing is to carve out time for employee interaction in your day or week. Also, make sure that everyone in HR knows what you are doing and when.

• Call new hires to make sure they received their health plan and prescription (Rx) ID cards, summaries of coverage, and summary plan descriptions

• Offer assistance enrolling in the mail-order Rx program

• Offer assistance finding a doctor or dentist

• Send out email alerts reminding plan participants to get a physical, eye exam, or dental cleaning

• Create an employee benefits newsletter

• Create an employee benefits Facebook page and blog

• Remind employees of available health care price transparency tools so that they can shop around for care (especially if you offer a Health Savings Account (HSA))

• Remind employees to start or increase retirement plan contributions

• Do interesting things that people enjoy and look forward to, like mini benefits fairs throughout the year (These do not have to be extravagant— you can invite your health plan services manager to one fair with the rest of the benefits staff to answer general employee questions)

You get the idea. And it's not just about you, surveys show that employees want to speak more often about benefits too.

One Step Forward, Two Steps Back – Feeling Overwhelmed

"If we can't find the way forward, let's find the way back."

I'm more than knee-deep into writing this Guide and think you may be overwhelmed. So far, my message is: to be a *Benefits Know It All*, you need to be smart. Read and write great stuff. Communicate effectively. Gather and use great resources and references. Ignore toxic colleagues and embrace ambiguity. Know All.

I can see how reading all of that would make you want to choose a different career. How much do benefit pros make anyway? I'm not touching that one.

So how can we get back to simple? Easy. It's okay to copy what others have done before (if their work was good). It's also okay to ask for help.

I. Copy, Study, Improve

Most of us learn by doing, and some of us do things without learning. The workplace is full of people saying and doing things they don't really understand. Now I'm not hating on these folks, but I can recognize when someone is talking about or doing something they don't quite comprehend. Mainly because they cannot answer the most basic question, "Why are we doing this?" They know the "how" but not the "why" of their actions.

As I said before, *I'm not mad at them.* I know the feeling of doing something without fully understanding it. It's a feeling that nearly every employee benefits professional experiences at least once. You see, we are often asked to do things with little or no instruction beforehand. Our boss can't help because he doesn't know how to do it or doesn't want to take the time to teach us, and the person who did it last is either gone or not interested in helping.

So how do you learn and not just do technical work with little or no assistance? You check out what was done before, copy it, and study it. Copy before you study? Yes. Sometimes you just need to do the task and worry about understanding it later. But if you do have time to study before copying, do that. For example:

Filing Form 5500 for Health & Welfare and Retirement Plans

Background

Federal law (ERISA and the Internal Revenue Code) requires employers with a certain number of employees participating in their health insurance or retirement plans at the start of a plan year to file Form 5500. The Department of Labor, Internal Revenue Service, and the Pension Benefits Guaranty Corporation created Form 5500 jointly. The Form serves numerous purposes and provides information to many groups.

For example, Congress and the White House can use aggregate Form 5500 data to estimate the annual loss of federal tax revenue due to participation in tax-favored health insurance and retirement plans. They can also determine who needs access to these plans and decide what policies to put in place to address the needs of these people.

In sum, Form 5500 is a compliance document that assures benefit pros administer benefit plans in accordance with the law. Also, it is a valuable research tool for the public and private sectors.

Confession: First-timer

One year, the CFO of our company decided his office would no longer prepare Form 5500 for the health and welfare benefit plans. The VP of HR, who was responsible for the administration of the plans, now had to prepare the annual filing. Which meant I had to prepare it. Preparing the Form was a first for me, but I knew that if I could view a previous filing, I could figure out what to do. To prepare the form, I did the following.

• I requested copies of the filings from the CFO, but they were sparse and incomplete (they neglected to make copies of the Schedules)

• I read everything available on the DOL website about Form 5500 and what data I needed to include on the Form

• I discovered a valuable, free online resource called freeerisa.com with a database of prior years' 5500 filings from just about any company that filed (the service is now freeerisa.benefitspro.com). I downloaded and printed our firm's previous five (5) years of filings. I also reviewed the Form 5500s of our competitors

• I emailed our insurers to request the Schedules I needed to prepare the Form (they are supposed to send these automatically or let you know when they are available for digital download, but sometimes you have to contact them). How did I know what Schedules I needed? The digital version of the prior year's filing included the Schedules and the contact information of the entity and person who prepared it. The Form 5500 instructions on the DOL website also told me what info I needed and where to get it

• I copied the information from the previous year's Form 5500 and added the updated participant count and dollar values; but mostly, I copied

• I wrote a procedure for everything I did and stapled it to the front of the folder. I kept the complete copies of the filing. My instructions included how to register for freeerisa.com and gain access to previous filings

• I also discovered that our firm had made several mistakes on prior year filings that I was able to correct

Now, how hard was that!

II.   Ask For Help

I'm a natural-born giver. If I have the time, resources, or knowledge to help someone, I won't hesitate to assist them. You see, I don't have any insecurity about helping others succeed. I believe if you know how to do something or know of a resource to help someone reach their goals, you should tell them about it.

On the flip side, asking for help makes me feel incredibly vulnerable. I seek help occasionally, but it does not come naturally to me, and I should do it more often. There are two reasons I don't like asking for help. One, I want to figure out things on my own. Two, I've been made to feel like a burden when asking for help in the past. It's a stinging feeling.

Here are my rules for giving and seeking help.

Rules for Giving Help

Rule #1: Give without expecting anything in return. Quid pro quo (which means I give you something, and you give me something) is a rule too many follow nowadays. Some people won't entertain any request for help if it is not accompanied by a promise to return the favor immediately. Don't be one of these people.

Rule #2: Give without expecting anything in return. Quid pro quo (which means I give you something, and you give me something) is a rule too many follow nowadays. Some people will only entertain a request for assistance if it is accompanied by a promise to return the favor immediately. Don't be one of these people.

Rule #3: Do what you say you are going to do. Some people will say "yes" to a request for help and either forget about it or hope you forget about it. Follow through with all requests for help, even if your answer is "No."

Rule #4: Give timely. Who wants to wait around for you to get around to helping them? If you cannot grant a request soon, say so. Also, say when you will be able to help.

Rule #5: Don't give grudgingly. We all hate to ask someone for something, and they react in a defensive, hostile, or condescending manner. If you are going to help someone, do it with a smile, or don't do it at all.

Rules for Receiving Help

Rule #1: Ask for precisely what you want/need and nothing more. No one likes to receive a vague request that requires guessing what you want. Also, no one likes to receive a huge request that requires a lot of time and resources.

Rule #2: Don't put people on the spot. Make your request for assistance in private, if possible. Some people may feel they have no choice but to help you if you ask when others are around. That goes for email, too—don't "copy" other people when requesting help from one person.

Rule #3: Don't get emotional. Showing too much emotion in any situation can make most people feel uncomfortable. They would have granted your request if you didn't get all weird on them. Now they just want to run away from you and never see or hear from you again. Be professional.

Rule #4: Be prepared to have your request rejected or ignored. Not everyone wants to help you, not even a little bit. Some people may feel taken advantage of when someone asks them for help. No matter how small the request. Or they feel like they did it on their own, and you should too (of course, no one does it on their own). Don't take it personally; that's just who they are!

Rule #5: Don't think the worst of people because they decline or ignore your request for help. They may have a legitimate reason for not helping. People are busy doing their own work and living their own lives. They may feel that they don't have the time or resources to help someone else.

Hopefully, taking a step back has calmed your nerves, and you are again ready to become a *Benefits Know It All.*

The Stage Is Yours Benefit Pros

There will always be something new to learn in employee benefits. Health care reform, health insurance plan technology and retirement plan access, fees, and fiduciary issues are topics benefit pros will tackle in the foreseeable future. Rely on your continuous research and reading habits to help you keep track of the latest things you need to know and address. But in the meantime, take the opportunity to showcase the knowledge and skills you already have. Hosting health and wellness fairs, new hire employee benefits orientations, and annual benefits open enrollment is your time to shine.

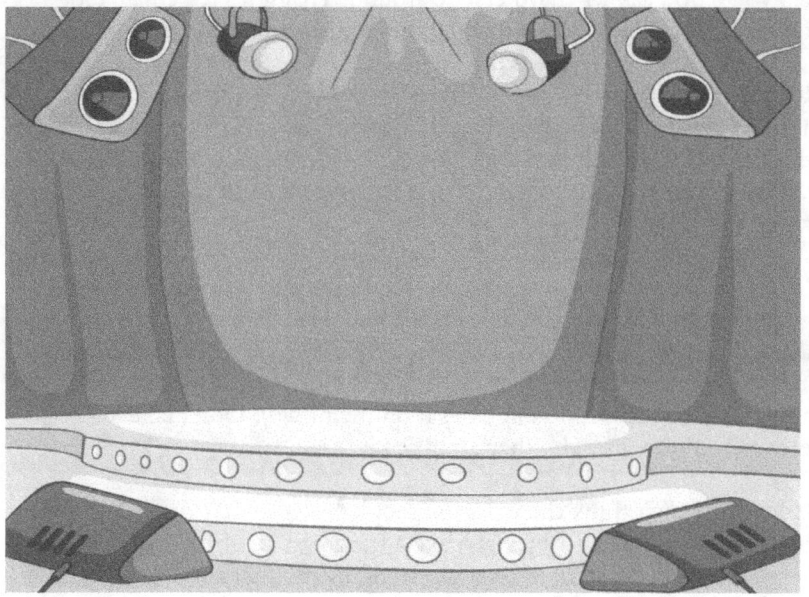

Yeah, it would help if you communicated different aspects of your organization's benefits program throughout the year. But we already talked about how that is easier said than done. You know, with senior HR management trying to keep the benefits function hidden until open enrollment time. This interference is why you must take maximum advantage of the *annual events that spotlight what you have to offer*.

Health and Wellness Fairs

Who doesn't like to attend a good fair? There is always great food, prizes, and various activities to engage in. Unfortunately, this is how too many employee benefits offices approach the annual health and wellness fair. It is an opportunity to put on a good show and entertain employees. This exercise of style versus substance is not always intentional. Sometimes it just happens. I should know because it happened to me.

Giveaways, Food, and Activities

My first experience leading a workplace health and wellness fair was in the late 1990s. The '90s were when CEOs and CFOs openly rejected wellness programs because of their inability to show any positive return on investment (ROI). Today, health and wellness programs are part of most employee benefits budgets. Back to the event...

With a committee of employee volunteers, we *hosted a fall health and wellness fair that was textbook perfect*.

• Committee members arranged for food, prizes, and facility decorations

• Local businesses donated prizes like athletic sneakers and apparel, gym membership discounts, free meals at local restaurants, free massages, and more. We collected enough free prizes to give every employee at least one. And I am not talking about those insurance company giveaways like chip clips and toothbrushes, but we had those too.

• Committee members cooked the food, which included healthy fall soups, a ton of vegetable lasagna, baked chicken curry egg rolls, roast turkey and cheese sandwiches, and a few other items.

• Committee members decorated the venue. The fall theme decorations met you at the door of the facility. They continued throughout—a "Welcome To Wellness" banner, bales of hay, fall flowers, pumpkins, and other squash sitting on seasonal blankets. Our workplace had a large facility with a gymnasium and kitchen, allowing all our employees to attend the fair together.

• We invited outside participants like health insurance company reps, third-party administrators, and individuals from the local wellness and fitness communities, including Weight Watchers and the American Heart

Association. Insurance representatives did biometric screenings and answered general plan questions. A yogi put on yoga demonstrations. Two local massage therapists provided free massages.

Great Success or Epic Fail

Even though no health and wellness-related objectives were set before or measured after the event, by all accounts, the fair was a smashing success. It was the first-ever health and wellness fair the company hosted, and even the most difficult-to-please employees said it was the best event the company ever offered. Ever! Our insurance company reps said it was the best benefits/wellness fair they had ever attended. Ever! The head of the organization raved about the fair in a senior staff meeting, citing its meager cost and great reception by employees.

Even though my opinion on workplace wellness programs has changed, I'm still proud of hosting this event. Employees like these events, and a successful one can enhance the reputation of the benefits department.

New Hire Benefits Orientation

Many employees have a negative opinion of the new hire orientation, especially the employee benefits session. They're too long, too dull, and just too much! As one of the cast of HR characters charged with meting out this torture, you may either love or hate the program. Meanwhile, new hires would likely only review benefits information and submit enrollment forms on time if they were told to during orientation.But then again, the primary purpose of the new hire orientation is not to collect paperwork. At least, it should not be. Sure, that is an important function of the process, but the main point is to help employees make well-informed financial decisions about health insurance and retirement savings. So, take the task seriously if your job requires you to host the new hire benefits orientation. It is a new hire's first opportunity to judge you and the benefits department. A poor "performance" will never be forgotten, nor will a good one. To make it a good one:

Attend a Colleague's Employee Benefits Orientation

• As a new employee benefits professional, your training may include watching a supervisor or coworker lead a new hire benefits orientation. You can learn a lot from this training. The key is to look for things worth incorporating into your future orientations and items you want to avoid.

• Some employee benefits are more confusing than others. Pay special attention to how new hires react to these segments of the orientation. Do they look confused? Do they ask questions? Revise these segments to make them easier to understand.

• Also, pay attention to the rhythm and tone of the session. Is it engaging? At what stage of the orientation do employees begin to lose interest? Answering these questions may give you an idea of how much time you should devote to the orientation. Should it be 30, 45, or 60 minutes long or longer?

• Watching others lead a new hire benefits orientation provides valuable lessons on what to do, what not to do, what to cover, and for how long.

Read Everything –

The following information almost repeats what I said at the beginning of this Guide, but it bears repeating.

Before conducting my first new hire benefits orientation, I memorized the two-page benefit plan summaries prepared by the insurers for our medical, dental, life, and disability insurance plans; and the plan booklet prepared by the retirement plan administrator. These documents comprised all the information provided to me by my supervisor, so I assumed it was all that I needed and all that was available.

The first few benefits orientations went well. I appeared to know what I was talking about and could answer all questions thrown my way. That is until someone asked me what 401(k) stood for. I told him it was a type of retirement plan that the firm offered in addition to our defined benefits pension plan. That is correct, but it did not answer his question. I told him its mechanics when he cut me off and said, "Yeah, but what does it mean."

I am no dummy. I immediately detected that this person knew what 401(k) stood for and knew that I did not. Of course, he was happy to tell me and all the other new hires that it referred to Section 401(k) of the Internal Revenue Code. I lightened the mood with a joke, ten days out of college, you would think I would know everything.

I knew I had to learn more. I discovered the plan documents and summary plan descriptions (SPD) that provided detailed information about the plans, including what was not covered. I also read old plan brochures, open enrollment, and other benefits program announcements to see how the firm's benefits program evolved. The number of employees who do not know their health plan enrollment status is surprising.

The best way to prepare for a benefits orientation is to read all of the plan documentation. Reading general health insurance and financial information from government and private online publications and websites is also a good idea. There is no shortage of related newsletters, RSS feeds, and blogs you can subscribe to.

Listen Up –

Even after conducting benefits orientations for years, you may get nervous before each session. Public speaking is a fear shared by many people. So, allow for some nerves, but rely on your knowledge and desire to help others overcome your fears. Also, consider that new hires are just as excited as you are. Chances are they are learning about health and life insurance and retirement plans for the first time and may find the material intimidating. It's your job to make them feel relaxed and ready to learn.

And one of the best ways to set a relaxing mood is to smile. (Seriously, it works.) Not only will smiling relieve your stress, but it will also convey to others that you are happy and confident, which may, in turn, make them feel the same way. However, you may want to smile only a little, as it can have the opposite effect. It can make others feel uncomfortable and make you look foolish.

A new hire benefits orientation is not a funeral service. If your presentation is stiff and stoic, employees may struggle to concentrate on what you are communicating. Create a professional but friendly and engaging atmosphere (conversational) for every orientation.

Provide Examples and Comparisons —

Most benefit professionals are taught to recite a general laundry list of health and retirement plan rules and definitions as the central part of the benefits orientation. I was as guilty as the next employee benefits pro of waiting for a new hire to ask a specific question before providing a real-world example of how Plan A works in a given situation. Not providing these examples and comparisons upfront is one of the main reasons new hire benefits orientations are unsuccessful.

New hires cannot possibly decide which health plan to choose or how to calculate their approximate out-of-pocket costs by listening to a list of what's covered and deductible, coinsurance, and copay amounts. They need an example using a specific health care occurrence. Fortunately, the new Summary of Benefits Coverage (SBC) documents required by the Affordable Care Act for all health plans provide these types of coverage examples and comparisons. There are also online coverage calculators to calculate the out-of-pocket costs of different plans.

When reviewing benefit plan information, provide examples of how the benefits work in the real world. Don't just recite a list of benefit plan features.

Follow-up —

After the new hire benefits orientation, you should follow up with new hires to remind them to make a benefit plan election or ask if they have any questions. Many benefit pros grumble about performing this task because they fail to understand the value of following up. To them, it is all about collecting paperwork and processing benefit plan elections. They need to see it as an opportunity to answer specific questions so the employee can better understand their options. In other words, the follow-up is where the real education takes place.

Following up with new hires after the benefits orientation is as important as the orientation itself. Consider scheduling a one-on-one session with new hires to answer their specific questions and help them make their benefits elections. These follow-up meetings may seem like a doubling of the work, but they could save time and effort. It will also enhance your professional reputation and positively influence employees' feelings about their benefits.

Annual Benefits Open Enrollment

When just about anyone thinks of the workplace employee benefits function, they think of the annual benefits open enrollment. It is the Super Bowl in primetime, or, for us tennis fans, it's Serena Williams in the U.S. Open final. Seriously, it's a big deal. Benefits pros are treated like rock stars for two to six weeks each year. We pull out our collection of benefits communication's greatest hits, and things start humming. And like all bad rock stars, we think we are killing it.

The reality is there are a lot of obstacles to overcome just to get the show on the road.

Three Open Enrollment Challenges: Time, Cost, and Communication

<u>Time</u>: Employees don't know this, but the open enrollment period starts with the insurance renewal process. The renewal process is when the top HR and benefits staff sits down with their medical plan insurance reps to agree on premiums and plan benefits. Ancillary plans like dental, vision, and flexible spending accounts don't usually require face-to-face renewal meetings. These "negotiations" take place via email. (It's another ballgame if you are introducing a new benefit plan.)

The renewal period typically occurs late in the plan year, and employers must compete with each other for the attention of their insurance representatives. Additionally, employers and insurers want to include as much of the current year's claims data in the renewal quote as possible. The more data the quote includes the more valid and reliable the cost and premium projections. All this waiting and back-and-forth negotiating limits the time HR must prepare for and hold the open enrollment period.

<u>Cost</u>: Cost is always an obstacle in any negotiation—one side wants to keep it low, and the other wants to make sure they make a profit. Insurers rely on their actuaries to project the coming year's health insurance costs. And because they place so much faith in these projections, they are reluctant to reduce their original quote. Employers are limited by their

annual budgets and must find ways to keep cost increases to a minimum. Once the two sides agree on a price, next comes the difficult task of deciding how much the employer will pay and how much employees will pay. These decisions must occur before preparing any open enrollment communications.

Communication: How much more can I say about the challenges of employee benefits communication?

Employees don't care about all the work that goes into rolling out the annual open enrollment. They want to know what health and other insurance plans are available for the coming year, the covered benefits, the doctors and medical facilities that accept them, and how much they will cost. Consequently, and at a minimum, open enrollment communication should clearly address all of these questions.

But answering these questions is just the beginning. Creating a new open enrollment communications plan is essential to make this event successful for employees and the benefits function.

Some benefits communication experts suggest creating different communications based on employee demographics. You could do that, but I prefer creating multiple medical care-related scenarios. For example, offer a scenario of someone getting a knee replacement or having a baby. Include the annual premium cost, deductible, coinsurance, and copay amounts.

Having A Baby: Plan Name and Type

• **Deductible**: $5,000 (what will the deductible be if the pregnancy crosses over to a second calendar year…)

• **Coinsurance**: You pay: 20% in-network; 40% out-of-network

• **Copay**: You pay: $30

• **Estimated Cost of Prenatal Care**: (get info from broker or insurer or use a health care price calculator that includes your geographical area):

• **Estimated Cost of Vaginal Birth**:

• **Estimated Cost of Cesarean** (C-section):

• **Total estimated cost** (no complications):

• **Coverage for nontraditional services** (doula, midwife, or water birth): Yes/No

Work with your broker or insurance representative to provide relevant cost scenarios based on claims data. Focus on common medical issues like back problems and allergies. It's a lot of work, but once you do it, you only have to update the numbers annually. Make sure you use only reputable data sources. Stress that the scenarios are estimates, and actual costs may be higher or lower—you probably want to include this note at the top and bottom of the scenario and in between. Cautious!

Employee benefit pros don't participate in a lot of company-wide events. That is why it is important to show the company what a valuable resource the benefits function is during Open Enrollment. Health and wellness fairs, new hire benefits orientations, and annual open enrollment are golden moments for benefit pros. Handle them well, and you will be a superstar, but the reverse is also true.

In addition to company-wide benefits events that allow you to show your worth, there is the all-important everyday task of helping employees resolve benefits claim issues.

Claims, Claims, Everywhere There's Claims...

Job Security

Employee benefit professionals often assist employees in resolving disputes over denied or improperly paid insurance claims. These encounters are the most one-on-one contact benefit pros have with employees. Therefore, it is important that these interactions are handled with professionalism and understanding.

To make sure that happens create a checklist or mini guide you can use every time you assist with a claim dispute. Or use an existing checklist or guide and modify it for your needs. Check out the guide from the *Kaiser Family Foundation: A Consumer Guide to Handing Disputes With Your Employer Or Private Health Plan (2005 Update)*.

The first step to any guide on claims disputes should include how to prevent a claim dispute from happening in the first place and the final step of filing an appeal with the State Department of Insurance. You can share these customized guides with employees, in the form of a brochure, as part of the new hire employee benefits package, as a newsletter article, or on the company website (or all of these).

Creating a claims dispute resolution guide or checklist is not difficult; working with an upset and confused employee is. Therefore, it is important to know what to expect and establish some guidelines and expectations for the employee and you.

What to Expect From an Employee Disputing an Insurance Claim

• Expect them to be upset
• Expect them to talk too fast
• Expect them to leave out relevant information
• Expect them to want you to agree with them
• Expect them to want an immediate resolution

Guidelines for Assisting an Employee With an Insurance Claim Dispute

•**Don't** speculate as to why the claim was not paid

•**Don't** promise that the claim will be paid

•**Don't** agree or disagree with anything the employee has to say

•**Do** ask the employee to fill out a HIPAA Authorization form

•**Do** gather as much information about the claim as possible including date of service, name of treating physician, name and full address of medical facility/doctor's office, type of service, new or continuing treatment

•**Do** set aside a time to contact your designated insurance company representative for assistance

•**Do** closely review the Appeal procedures of the insurance plan document for procedural reference and appeal time limits

•**Do** follow up with the employee at least once daily (email is fine unless the employee requests a call or visit) with the status of your intervention

•**Do** require the employee to contact the medical provider's billing office to inform them of the claim dispute and ask them not to send the claim to a collection agency

It is important to recognize that the employee or their dependent is concerned or upset about the claim. You can acknowledge their feelings but don't make promises you can't keep because you want to make them feel better.

My technique (Conversational): *I understand that these insurance claims issues can be frustrating. Also, Explanation of Benefits (EOB) statements can be challenging to understand. I am going to ask a few questions so that I can get a clear understanding of what we are dealing with before I contact my plan representative. I may ask about a few obvious things you already told me; I just want to be clear on all the details. So, let's try to get this issue resolved. Also, let's agree that what we are trying to resolve is to make sure that the plan paid everything it was supposed to pay in accordance with the policy.*

Learning From Each Claim Dispute Intervention

Employee benefit professionals often complain about employees not reading and understanding their health and retirement benefits package. Assuming all your benefits communications are understandable is a big mistake. Every time an employee seeks your help is an opportunity to improve how you design and communicate your benefits program.

Assisting employees with insurance claim disputes is important for several reasons, including but not limited to:

• It is an opportunity to help an employee with a specific need
• It is an opportunity to re-educate employees about plan benefits
• It is an opportunity to audit the claims processing procedures of the insurer or TPA
• It is an opportunity to enhance the reputation and credibility of the benefits function

Other Claim Dispute Considerations

You be on your toes when assisting with an insurance claim dispute. You have to determine the facts of the specific claim at hand. At the same time, you have to manage the emotions of the affected employee. Added to that, you have to consider other issues that may come up during this process.

Dealing with a medical provider/facility insurance billing office. One of the first steps in assisting an employee with a claim dispute involves contacting the medical provider's billing office. The employee should make the call. They can do this in your presence or on their own. The call serves as a heads-up to the medical provider's billing office that a claim is in dispute and not to expect payment at this time. Ask the billing representative to refrain from sending the claim to a collection agency while you work with the insurer to determine who should pay the bill.

TIP: Few doctors have in-house billing operations; most outsource this function. Contact the medical provider or medical facility to inquire who handles their insurance billing and call that person.

Dealing with a collection agency. Many employees will wait until a medical claim has been sent to a collection agency before they seek your assistance. Often an employee thinks that they can handle the matter alone or think it is a mistake that the doctor's office will eventually work out with the insurer. However, some provider billing offices have a fixed schedule for submitting a claim for collection. They may send the claim to collections before the employee can resolve it independently.

Legitimate denials – Not eligible for benefits. It is a hard pill to swallow for employees, but sometimes a claim dispute is not decided in their favor for the simplest reasons. Explore these reasons first by reviewing the claim's Explanation of Benefits (EOB) statement and the plan document.

• The medical services required preauthorization by the insurer before receipt

• The employee or employee's dependent is not eligible to receive benefits because of age, reaching the maximum allowed benefits, using a non-participating provider, etc.

Unique plan designs. Insurance plans often have standard benefits. So, when an employer requests a unique benefit that is not part of a standard insurance contract, this language needs to be added to the claims system as an override to process claims for this unique benefit.

For example, an insurer offers all of its clients a particular plan with a specific plan design and network of providers that have a $1,000 deductible, 30% coinsurance, and $35 office visit copay. You, the employer, request the same plan but change the coinsurance amount to 20%--sounds like a minor change (20% instead of 30%). However, that insurer has to update several of its computer systems and include special instructions in its claims systems to make sure your group's claim process is in accordance with your contract. The claim may be denied if even one part of the system is not updated with the "unique" benefits.

When to Back Out of a Claim Dispute

Insurers routinely process most claim disputes within minutes, hours, or days. But others are not. Once you have done all you can to assist an employee with a claim, and they remain dissatisfied with the result, it's time they submit a formal appeal. The plan's appeal process is outlined in the health plan document. Employees may also contact their State Department of Insurance to appeal a claim.

With claims disputes, time is of the essence. Create a claims disputes file and set aside at least one hour each workday to address any outstanding claim issues.

Conclusion

Being a *Benefits Know It All* means continuous, often self-directed learning; feeling comfortable working in a world of grays; finding a way to say "yes," and picking a side on issues that affect the benefits world. Use this Guide to learn about creating habits to increase your knowledge of workplace employee benefits.

When I started my career in employee benefits, I had no idea what to expect. I didn't have access to the many online resources available today. So, like most new professionals, I dealt with things at work as they came. Every task was a separate operation to perform and store in the memory bank. I could have continued to "learn" my profession this way but chose a different route. I decided to go searching for knowledge to supplement my on-the-job experiences.

It all started with reading every word of every employee benefits document my employer had. Reading this information led me to even more employee benefits resources. I also paid close attention to what the benefit pros around me were doing and saying. I found that meetings with third-party vendors and service providers help me understand routine and complex benefits matters. I also placed great importance on keeping up with benefits case law. Knowing how the courts interpreted the many benefits laws, regulations, and statutes helped shape my approach to administering benefits programs and avoiding liability for my employers.

Another thing I learned early in my employee benefits career was the power of using technology to perform routine tasks. Using technology meant consistency and accuracy. Technology also freed up time to create procedures, and checklists/calendars, improve work processes, focus on the more difficult benefits issues like leave management, and assist employees with benefits claim issues.

The thought of approaching my work as disjointed tasks or having a cursory understanding of what I was doing was never an option. Honestly, I never thought much about my all-embracing approach to employee benefits management until much later in my career. I realized my approach to learning and performing my job was different. This comprehensive approach to work made me feel more comfortable questioning the status quo. I started to think more about how the insurance and financial services industries and public policy impacted my profession. And I had an opinion about it. I want every benefit pro to have an opinion about what they do, which starts with a deep knowledge of the employee benefits function. Because what's the point of being a Benefits Know It All if you don't share your thoughts and opinions?

Resources

•http://www.npr.org/sections/health-shots/2015/06/16/414665468/defeat-by-deductible-millennials-arent-hip-to-health-insurance-lingo

• http://www.benefitspro.com/2015/10/16/half-of-millennials-cant-define-deductible

•https://www.dol.gov/ebsa/pdf/rdguide.pdf

•http://www.brightscope.com

•http://kff.org/health-reform/poll-finding/assessing-americans-familiarity-with-health-insurance-terms-and-concepts/

•http://nautil.us/blog/your-speech-is-packed-with-misunderstood-unconscious-messages

•https://nces.ed.gov/pubs93/93275.pdf

•http://www.kaizen.com/about-us/definition-of-kaizen.html

•https://www.towerswatson.com/en/Press/2015/12/surveys-reveal-disconnect-between-retirees-and-employers-over-retirement-medical-benefits

•https://www.medicare.gov/Pubs/pdf/02179.pdf

•http://www.ehow.com/how_5608_resolve-claim-dispute.html, https://kaiserfamilyfoundation.files.wordpress.com/2005/07/7350consu merguidev4_080805.pdf

Employee Benefits Surveys

Employee benefits administration relies heavily on administrative, legal and compliance advice, benchmarking, and tracking of trends. Below are lists of employee benefits administration resources including surveys, reference manuals, books, professional associations, etc. This is not an exhaustive compilation of available resources nor is it an endorsement of any of the resources listed. The materials listed were compiled from multiple online sources and other publications.

Benefit pros use the below resources to:

• Learn what their competitors are doing or plan to do
• Learn what benefits employees want and don't want
• Compare benefits programs and program costs
• Make recommendations to senior management for benefits program changes

Who conducts benefits surveys: public policy groups, employee benefits consulting groups, professional associations/benefits advocacy groups, unions, government agencies, and private companies.

Surveys

Aon Hewitt: *Trends & Experience in Defined Contribution Plans* (Biennial)
Greenwich Associates: *United States Investment Management Market Trends* (Annual)
Arthur J. Gallagher & Co.: *Benefits Strategy and Benchmarking Survey* (Annual)
Bureau of Labor Statistics (BLS): *Employee Benefits Survey* (Annual) and *National Compensation Survey* (Annual)
CUPA-HR: *Healthcare Benefits in Higher Education Survey* (Annual)

Economic Research Institute (ERI): *Health Care Benefits Benchmarking Survey* (Annual)

Employee Benefits Research Institute (EBRI) Employee Benefits Surveys:

> *EBRI/Greenwald & Associates Consumer Engagement in Health Care Survey*
>
> *EBRI Health and Voluntary Workplace Benefits Survey*
>
> *EBRI Retirement Confidence Survey*

Office of Personnel Management (OPM): *Federal Employee Benefits Survey* (Annual)

IFEBP Research Surveys: *Employee Benefits Surveys* (Annual)

Mercer: *National Survey of Employer-Sponsored Health Plans* (Annual)

MetLife: *Employee Benefits Trends Survey* (Annual)

Plan Sponsor Council of America: *Annual Survey of Profit Sharing and 401(k) Plans* (Annual)

Society Human Resources Management (SHRM): *Employee Benefits Research Report* (Annual)

Henry J. Kaiser Family Foundation (KFF): *Employer Health Benefits Survey* (Annual)

Towers Watson: *Voluntary Benefits and Services Survey* (Annual)

Transamerica (TCRS): *Annual Transamerica Retirement Survey* (Annual)

Willis Towers Watson: *Accounting for Pensions and Other Postretirement Benefits: Reporting Under U.S. GAAP Among the Fortune 1000 Companies* (Annual)

National Association of Government Defined Contribution Administrators, Inc.: *Survey of Defined Contribution Plans* (Annual)

Employee Benefits References

Regularly updated reference sources used to design, set up, and maintain health and welfare, flexible benefits, and pension and retirement savings plans.

References (italicized links represent the latest available publications as of 07/2017) –

401(k) Answer Book by Empower Retirement (Wolters Kluwer Law & Business)

403(b) Answer Book by Barbara N. Seymon-Hirsch and Janet M. Anderson-Briggs (Wolters Kluwer Law & Business)

457 Answer Book by Gary S. Lesser, David W. Powell, and Peter J. Gulia (Wolters Kluwer Law & Business)

Annual Report – (Pension Benefits Guaranty Corporation (PBGC))

Civil Service Retirement and Disability Fund Annual Report – CSRDF Annual Reports (Office of Personnel Management-OPM)

COBRA Handbook by Ira M. Golub and Roberta K. Chevlowe (Wolters Kluwer Law & Business)

Employee Benefits Answer Book by Dorinda D. DeScherer (Wolters Kluwer Law & Business)

Employee Fringe and Welfare Benefits Plans by Michael J. Canan and William Mitchell (Thomson West)

ERISA: A Comprehensive Guide by Paul J. Schneider and Brian M. Pinheiro (Wolters Kluwer Law & Business)

Flexible Benefits Answer Book by Bernadine Topazio (Wolters Kluwer Law & Business)

Governmental Plans Answer Book by Carol V. Calhoun, Cynthia L. Moore, and Keith Brainard (Wolters Kluwer Law & Business)

Health Insurance Answer Book by John C. Garner (Wolters Kluwer Law & Business)

Multistate Guide to Benefits Law by John F. Buckley IV (Wolters Kluwer Law & Business)

Pension Distribution Answer Book by Carol R. Sears, Scott D. Miller, and Melanie N. Aska (Wolters Kluwer Law & Business)

Pension Planning: Pension, Profit-Sharing, and Other Deferred Compensation Plans by Everett T. Allen et al. (Irwin/McGraw-Hill)

Qualified Retirement Plans by Michael J. Canan and Charles Shulman (Thomson West)

The Handbook of Employee Benefits: Health and Group Benefits by Jerry S. Rosenbloom (McGraw-Hill)

The Pension Answer Book by Stephen J. Krass (Wolters Kluwer Law & Business, Published annually)

U.S. Master Employee Benefits Guide (Wolters Kluwer Law & Business, Annual)

Subscription Publications (aka loose leaf service – periodic updates)

The 401(k) Handbook by Arris R. Murphy and Paul M. Hamburger (Thompson HR)

Employer's Handbook: Complying with IRS Employee Benefits Rules by Todd A. Solomon, David R. Fuller (Thompson HR)

Employer's Guide to Fringe Benefits Rules by David R. Fuller and Vicki M. Nielsen (Thompson HR)

Employer's Guide to HIPAA Privacy Requirements by Kathryn Bakich and Joanne Hustead (Thompson HR)

Employer's Guide to the Health Insurance Portability and Accountability Act by Mark L. Stember and Terry Humo (Thompson HR)

Flex Plan Handbook by Rich Glass (Thompson HR)

Mandated Health Benefits--The COBRA Guide by Paul M. Hamburger (Thompson HR)

Pension & Profit Sharing 2d (Thomson Reuters)

Spencer's Research Reports on Employee Benefits (Wolters Kluwer Legal & Regulatory U.S.)

Government Employee Benefits Resources

Federal government resources for benefits laws, regulations and agencies.

Agency for Healthcare Research and Quality (AHRQ) – *http://www.ahrq.gov*

Americans With Disabilities Act (ADA) – *http://www.ada.gov/q%26aeng02.htm*

Consolidated Omnibus Budget Reconciliation Act (COBRA) –

http://www.dol.gov/ebsa/publications/cobraemployee.html

Department of Labor (DOL) – *"The Pension and Welfare Benefits Administration*

(PWBA) is responsible for the administration and enforcement of Title I of the Employee

*Retirement Income Security Act of 1974 (**ERISA**) and the Federal Employees' Retirement*

*System Act of 1986 (**FERSA**)…"* – *http://www.dol.gov/general/topic/health-plans*

Employee Benefits Security Administration – *http://www.dol.gov/ebsa/*

Family and Medical Leave Act (FMLA) – *http://www.dol.gov/whd/fmla/*

Federal and state elected official contact information –

http://m.usa.gov/usa/Contact/Elected

Health Insurance Portability and Accountability Act (HIPAA)–

http://www.dol.gov/ebsa/faqs/faq_consumer_hipaa.html

Internal Revenue Service (IRS) – *https://www.irs.gov/Businesses/Small-Businesses-*
&-Self-Employed/Employee-Benefits

IRS Publication 15 – Circular E *https://www.irs.gov/uac/About-Publication-15*

IRS Publication 919 – *http://www.irs.gov/publications/p919/ar02.html*

Local officials and governments (cities, counties, townships) –

http://www.statelocalgov.net/

Medicare Benefits apply online for Medicare Benefits –

http://www.socialsecurity.gov/medicareonly/

Mini-COBRA (state) laws – *http://www.cobrahealth.com/statelawdirectory.htm*

Occupational Safety & Health Administration (OSHA) – *https://www.osha.gov*

Patient Protection And Affordable Care Reform Act –

http://www.healthcare.gov/law/index.html

Pension Benefits Guarantee Corporation (PBGC) – *http://www.pbgc.gov*

Social Security Retirement Benefits –

http://www.socialsecurity.gov/pgm/retirement.htm

Social Security Retirement Plan Estimator –

http://www.socialsecurity.gov/estimator/

Unemployment insurance – (Bottom of the page, choose the state you live in)

http://www.servicelocator.org/OWSLinks.asp

Workers' Compensation (WC) Insurance (by state) –

http://www.workerscompensation.com/workers_comp_by_state.php

401(k) plans – *http://www.401khelpcenter.com/Employee_index.html*

Government Surveys

Employee Benefits Trending Analysis 1996-2006 (U.S. Chamber of Commerce)

Employer Costs for Employee Compensation (U.S. Department of Labor, Bureau of Labor Statistics)

National Compensation Survey: Employee Benefits in the United States (U.S. Department of Labor, Bureau of Labor Statistics)

Employee Benefits Periodicals And Health Care Books

These sources have the latest information on employee benefits administration programs, innovations, case law, and health policy.

Journals/Periodicals

Benefits Magazine (International Foundation of Employee Benefits Plans-IFEBP)

Benefits Quarterly (International Society of Certified Employee Benefits Specialists-ISCEBS)

EBRI Issue Brief (Employee Benefits Research Institute)

Employee Benefits News (SourceMedia Inc.)

Employee Benefits Plan Review (Wolters Kluwer Law & Business)

Health Affairs (Project HOPE)

Pensions & Investments (Crain Communications, Inc.)

Social Security Bulletin (U.S. Social Security Administration)

WorldatWork Journal (WorldatWork)

Modern Books - Health Care and Health Care Reform

America's Bitter Pill: Money, Politics, Back-Room Deals, and the Fight to Fix Our Broken Healthcare System by Steven Brill (2015)

Sick: The Untold Story of America's Health Care Crisis---and the People Who Pay the Price by Jonathan Cohn (Published by Harper April 10th 2007)

Health Care Reform: What It Is, Why It's Necessary, How It Works by Jonathan Gruber

(Published by Hill and Wang December 20th 2011—first published August 30th 2011)

Reinventing American Health Care: How the Affordable Care Act will Improve our Terribly Complex, Blatantly Unjust, Outrageously Expensive, Grossly Inefficient, Error Prone System by Ezekiel J. Emanuel (Published by PublicAffairs March 4th 2014)

Overtreated: Why Too Much Medicine Is Making Us Sicker and Poorer by Shannon Brownlee, Published September 18th 2007 by Bloomsbury USA

Poverty and the Myths of Health Care Reform July 8, 2016, by Richard (Buz) Cooper, MD

Employee Benefits Associations

Employee Benefits Associations provide invaluable resources to benefit professionals in the private, public, and non-profit sectors. These Associations represent industry members, but non-members have access to the voluminous amount of information and services they provide. Benefit pros can access Association-sponsored continuing education, certifications, research studies, webinars, and seminars. These groups sponsor surveys, publish articles, books, and magazines, give professional awards, and advocate for employee benefits and public policy issues.

Employee Benefits Associations – General:

American Benefits Council – *http://www.americanbenefitscouncil.org*

Council on Employee Benefits (CEB) – *https://www.ceb.org/about/index.cfm*

Employee Benefits Planning Association (EBPA) – *http://www.ebpa.org/About*

Employee Benefits Research Institute (EBRI) – *https://www.ebri.org/about/facts/*

ERISA Industry Committee (ERIC) – *http://www.eric.org/about/*

Federal Employee Benefits Association (FEBA) – *https://fedemplben.org*

International Association of Employee Benefit Plans (IFEBP) – *https://www.ifebp.org/Pages/default.aspx*

International Employee Benefits Association (IEBA) – *http://www.ieba.org.uk*

International Personnel Management Association for Human Resources (public sector) – *http://www.ipma-hr.org*

National Human Resources Association (NHRA) – *https://www.humanresources.org/website/c/?page=about*

National Labor Relations Board (NLRB) – *https://www.nlrb.gov*

Reward and Employee Benefits Association (REBA) – *http://www.reba.global*

Society for Human Resource Management (SHRM) –

http://www.shrm.org/pages/default.aspx

WorldatWork – *http://www.worldatwork.org/home/html/home*

Worldwide Employee Benefits Network (WEB) – *https://webnetwork.org*

Retirement Plan Associations:

American Association of Retired Persons (AARP) – *http://www.aarp.org*

American Retirement Association – *http://usaretirement.org*

International City/County Management Association (public sector) –

http://www.icmarc.org/about-us.html

National Association of Retirement Plan Participants (NARPP) –

http://www.narpp.org

National Association of State Retirement Administrators (NASRA) –

http://www.nasra.org/about

National Institute of Pension Administrators (NIPA) –

http://www.nipa.org/?page=AboutNIPA

Plan Sponsor Council of America (PSCA) – *http://www.psca.org*

Retirement Industry Trust Association (RITA) – *http://www.ritaus.org*

The Conference Board – *https://www.conference-board.org/about/index.cfm?id=1980*

<u>Other Associations</u>:

American Dental Association (ADA) – *http://www.ada.org/en/*

American Management Association (AMA) – *http://www.amanet.org*

Professional Certifications And Designations

Certifications and Designations:

• **CEBS – Certified Employee Benefit Specialist –** https://cebs.wharton.upenn.edu
• **CBP – Certified Benefits Professional –** WorldatWork - https://worldatwork.org/search/Init?q=How%20To%20Page%20for%20Certification&sort=
• **AGI – Associate in General Insurance –** www.theinstitutes.org
• **ARM – Associate in Risk Management –** www.theinstitutes.org
• **CMS – Compensation Management Specialist –** www.ifebp.org
• **GBA – Group Benefits Associate –** www.ifebp.org
• **RPA – Retirement Plans Associate –** www.ifebp.org
• **SHRM-CP – Society for Human Resource Management Certified Professional –** www.shrm.org
• **SHRM-SCP – Society for Human Resource Management Senior Certified – Professional –** www.shrm.org

Other Insurance Professional Designations:

http://www.ambest.com/resources/BRProfessionalDesignations.pdf

BONUS Resources: For Free Sample Documents that make benefits administration easy and accurate, log on to www.mybenefitsall.com/Freebies.php and use Code: **2-2-2-9**.

More Employee Benefits Resources

Records Retention:

Health and Welfare Benefit Plans

http://www.psfinc.com/press/record-retention-for-health-and-welfare-benefits-plans

Retirement Plans

http://www.ascende.com/Insight-Knowledge/Advisories-Publications/Retirement-Plan-Records-Retention/

General:

Dictionaries – http://www.mybenefitsall.com/BenefitsTerminology.html
Health Care Price Tools –
http://www.mybenefitsall.com/HealthcarePriceTools.html
Life Events – http://www.mybenefitsall.com/LifeEventChecklist.html

Policy Research:

Center for Retirement Research Boston College
http://crr.bc.edu
Transamerica Center for Retirement Studies
https://www.transamericacenter.org/retirement-research
Rand Corporation
http://www.rand.org/topics/health-insurance.html
Kaiser Family Foundation
http://kff.org
Urban Institute
http://www.urban.org/policy-centers/health-policy-center
American Enterprise Institute
https://www.aei.org/policy/health-care/
Heritage Foundation
http://www.heritage.org/initiatives/health-care

www.ingramcontent.com/pod-product-compliance
Lightning Source LLC
Chambersburg PA
CBHW060349190526
45169CB00002B/543